The Beatles, The Bible & Manson

In just two years, a would-be Messiah used lyrics from the most popular Rock and Roll band and verses from the most read book to create an infamous cult. This "family" remained run-of-the-mill until…

August 16, 1969.

Exactly one week after the hideously bizarre Tate-LaBianca murders,

200 members of the Los Angeles Police Department including the SWAT team storm the ranch where the Manson Family is living and arrest everyone there…

Two days later, all 24 detainees are simply released. Why would the LAPD apprehend every guilty party in the most notorious murders the city has ever experienced and then just let them go?

The Beatles, The Bible & Manson

Reflecting Back with 50 Years of Perspective

★ ★ ★ ★ ★

by

Tim & Deb Smith

Pandamensional Solutions, Inc.

Mendon, New York

Published by Pandamensional Solutions, Inc., Mendon, NY

Cover design by Catarina Lena Carosa

Cover photo credits:
Ventura County and State of California (Manson)
United States Library of Congress's Prints and Photographs division

ISBN-10: 1-938465-07-5
ISBN-13: 978-1-938465-07-9

What Others Are Saying About Tim & Deb Smith's
The Beatles, The Bible & Manson

"You two don't shy away from anything. When you told me you were going to tackle this topic I was intrigued. But I had no idea that you would come up with such a creative approach. You manage to take on such a tragic tale and make the read so engaging and satisfying. From an educational perspective, every fact that anyone would need to know about this event you have included. That component is commensurate to your calling here. But what really puts this book over the top is the unique style. Just when the tension is so thick you would need one of Manson's machetes to cut through it, you break into a song, or a poem, or a limerick which somehow manages to manipulate the mood while advancing the story at the same time. Congratulations! Pun intended . . . you guys absolutely killed it on this one."
   ➢ Dr. Frederick J. Marra

"I LOVE IT!! Several of your lines have stuck with me since I read the book. I didn't truly understand the intriguing nuances of this until you described all these surreal circumstances. I love the poems/limericks . . . they are just the right hint of humor to pull off the black comedy genre."
   ➢ Educator Beth Thomas

"What I can say is that I enjoyed the story a ton, and was very interested in all the dots you connected throughout. Generally, I enjoy your style of writing, the chattily, ironic, alliterative approach. You see and point out nuances I wouldn't otherwise have thought about. Most of all, I say congratulations on a remarkable and thorough piece of writing"
   ➢ Superintendent of Schools Doug Hamlin

"There were times when I was scared, there were times when I was angry, and there were times I was laughing my ass off. Literally a cackling-out-loud, tears-running-down-my-cheek kind of laughter. If ever there was a book that is guaranteed to run you through the whole gamut of emotions, this is the one."
   ➢ Historian Mike McGory

For our parents:

You *knew we had it right,*
even when **We** *didn't.*

TABLE OF CONTENTS

Foreword.. xi
Acknowledgements xiii

1. STORYLINE SAMPLER..1
2. MOMMIE DEAREST, THE EARLY YEARS
   (1934-1967) 7
3. THE BEACH BOYS AND THE BEATLES
   (MARCH-AUGUST, 1967) 11
4. THE WHITE ALBUM GOES HELTER SKELTER
   (SEPTEMBER-DECEMBER, 1968) 17
5. THE NEW YEAR'S EVE MANIFESTO
   (NEW YEAR'S EVE, 1968) 21
6. DISSECTING THE WHITE ALBUM
   (DECEMBER 31, 1968-MARCH 23, 1970)..24
7. MURDER AND MAYHEM
   (JULY 25-AUGUST 7, 1969)..31
8. THE TATE MURDERS
   (AUGUST 8-9, 1969)...38
9. THE LABIANCA MURDERS
   (AUGUST 9-11, 1969) 44
10. THE INVESTIGATION BEGINS
    (AUGUST 9-16, 1969) 49
11. NEWSPAPERS AND TABLOIDS
    (AUGUST 17-SEPTEMBER 30, 1969)..57
12. FINALLY FIGURING OUT WHO DID IT
    (OCTOBER 10-DECEMBER 16, 1969) 63
13. THE TRIAL BEGINS
    (FEBRUARY 26-JUNE 15, 1970)..73
14. LOTSAPOPPA AND MORE
    (JUNE 16-JULY 24, 1970)..81
15. OPENING STATEMENT
    (JULY 24-26, 1970) 87
16. STAR WITNESS
    (JULY 27-AUGUST 3, 1970)..93
17. LINDA KASABIAN CONTINUES THE GOOD FIGHT
    (AUGUST 3, 1970-AUGUST 13, 1970)...99

18. TIT FOR TAT EXCHANGES
    (AUGUST 3-SEPTEMBER 11, 1970)..................................104
19. LEAPS OF FAITH
    (SEPTEMBER 11-OCTOBER 5, 1970) 113
20. ENDING THE TESTIMONY AS WELL AS THE HUGHES SAGA
    (NOVEMBER 16, 1970-JANUARY 15, 1971) 120
21. YOUR HONOR, WE HAVE A VERDICT
    (JANUARY 16-MARCH 25, 1971)..................................127
22. DEATH BE NOT PROUD
    (MARCH 29-OCTOBER 21, 1971) 134
23. SUMMING UP FAMILY MATTERS
    (OCTOBER 22, 1971-NOVEMBER 19, 2017) 138

BONUS CHAPTER 1: THE BEATLES AND THE BIBLE...............144
BONUS CHAPTER 2: CHARACTER BACKSTORIES 158
BONUS CHAPTER 3: THE STRIKE OF THE COBRA EFFECT 177

Footnotes 184
About the Authors 192

FOREWORD

By actor David Grant Wright

First of all, I think I should tell you that I had previously read at least one book on the Manson story, and I had seen several of Charlie's interviews, and a couple of documentaries too. To be honest, I thought I knew the Manson story pretty well, but after reading your book, I realized that I really didn't know shit. You are master researchers!

There were all kinds of nibbles and nuggets in there that I knew nothing about. I was truly blown away by the depth of your storytelling, and if that had been all I had gotten out of it, it still would have been well worth the read. I know you start off by saying that this isn't the definitive factual book on the whole event, but because of the accessibility and detail in your writing, to me, the engrossing pages turned out to be just that.

Mostly, your success has to do with your voice. You have written it from such a distinctly singular point of view, (and I don't know how two people collaborate to do that so well) a point of view that felt very everyman and universal, and yet, personable and intimate. I felt you were talking directly to me; at the same time you were speaking in a glib, and authoritative voice. It's really quite an amazing feat. It makes me want to read more and more of your work.

Maybe it's just because I find you two so fascinating in real life, I felt like I got a feel for you as narrators or storytellers by the end of the book. I like knowing who is telling me this story from the top. Sort of a Tim and Deb take you through this amazing journey. This is who we are, and this is what brought us to this subject.

Yes, even though the subject was Charles Manson, I was turning the page to see what you would surprise and stab me with next. Not since the old man from Nantucket has there been such classic limericks. It all combines to make you so much fun to read!

Thank you for letting me read this. I felt very honored since it hasn't, yet, been published. Now, I will go back and dive into the other pieces that you sent me. Take care you, kind, funny, talented and fascinating people!

ACKNOWLEDGEMENTS

We write a weekly feature for our local paper the *Mendon-Honeoye Falls-Lima Sentinel* which services the southern suburbs of Rochester, New York. We get the whole back page and our weekly contributions check in at about 1,500 words.

This book actually started as just half of a one-week feature. With whom did we have Charles Manson sharing the bill? It was to be none other than the talented and lovely Lizzie Borden. The connecting concept is completely clear. Our theme was to be murder trials arousing widespread controversy and heated public debate. Or if we get you hot when we flash all fancy and French, they would be "cause célèbre" trials.

Others of this ilk would include from the early 1900's – Bruno Hauptmann (Lindberg baby); through the late 1900's O.J. Simpson (murdered wife); to the 2000's Amanda Knox (Italian roommate). From Lucky Lindy to the Juice to Foxy Knoxy.

At any rate we were sitting on our 750-word foray into the Manson murders and as often is the case with us, shit happens, one thing leads to another, and a few months later we've written a 50,000 word book. Not that the topic is particularly heartwarming, but the bizarre characters and storyline seemed appropriate for our irreverent offbeat style, and the muses mesmerized our minds motivating this mass marketing of the murderous and maniacal Manson story.

The publisher of our newspaper, Chris Carosa, had been encouraging us for some time to write a book. While the idea always intrigued us, we didn't jump right on board because we were having too much fun on our foray flitting from one topic to another. In general, our column has covered an eclectic variety of topics including music, sports, travel, history and human interest.

ECLECTIC TOPICS – We've gone from the hamlet of Centerfield, NY (population 25) to New York City (population 8.6 million).

Musically we've covered artists ranging from the innocence of Olivia Newton John to the shock rock of Alice Cooper. In the animal world we've reined in everything from the swimming pigs of the Bahamas to the bat bombs of Japan. And in nearby Niagara Falls we've watched people die from the Love Canal disaster and live while going over the Falls in a barrel.

EASTER ISLAND & CHRISTMAS ISLAND ~ Geographically we have traveled from Easter Island to Christmas Island. While visiting Easter Island we covered a tit-for-tat exchange the territory had with its mother country of Chile. This prompted us to pose the question, "What exactly is tat? Where do I get some? And how can I turn it in for the other thing?"

BASEBALL BIZARRERIE ~ In sports we have tackled topics from the absurd to the awesome. We told the story of how in 1951 the St. Louis Browns mocked Major League Baseball by sneaking Eddie Gaedel onto their roster, a midget who managed to get on base with a walk in his only appearance before being banned by baseball. On the other side of the spectrum we told the story of the late 1970's New York Yankees Bronx Zoo dynasty. Epitomizing the in-house histrionics of this team was the exchange when Mickey Rivers' response to being informed that his hated teammate Reggie Jackson had an IQ of 165 was to say, "Out of what, a thousand?"

HALLOWED HOLIDAYS ~ When it comes to holidays, we've celebrated all the ones you know and some of the ones you've never heard of. For example, Dyngus Day, which is a heavenly hearty and hallowed holiday highlighting our home turf of Upstate New York, is essentially to Poland what St. Patrick's Day is to Ireland. While we never need an excuse for drinking and debauchery, even if you've never heard of Dyngus Day, how can you not love a holiday where the romantic foreplay associated with the celebration consists of girls whipping wet boys with pussy willows? Is that not just dripping with symbolism, or what?

TIM & DEB'S TOTALLY TWISTED ROUTE 15 FUN FORAY ~ In our travels up and down the east coast we came to realize that on the 1,568 mile trek from Canada to Key West there is a 72-mile stretch on Route 15 in Pennsylvania where you're not on an expressway and merchants can lure in travelers who can view their retail establishments without having to exit the highway. Because that scenario is so rare, this stretch of road has become populated by a bizarrely quirky menagerie of merchants. Based on this we created a game travelers could play in their cars which we called Deb & Tim's Totally Twisted Route 15 Fun Foray. Check out our opening paragraph:

If you've ever fantasized about dressing up like an Indian and having sex under the fireworks then, for you, Route 15 south of Williamsport, Pennsylvania might just be a little slice of heaven right here on Earth. Since we've just nailed your sexual fantasies to a "T", we're sure that some of you are wondering how we've managed to peek into your bedroom window or hack into your computer. Well, don't feel bad, the Indian fireworks thing has been on our Top 10 list for many moons.

AUNT HELEN IN HEAVEN ~ One of our favorite real-life characters was Deb's Aunt Helen who passed away in 2017 at the age of 94. Funeral plans were unsettled; at one point some of Deb's family in Virginia were going to come up, but that all fell through and basically we could just pick a date, drive up, and have the service. So at that point, knowing that we were going to do the 5-hour New York drive from Rochester to Saranac Lake anyway, and also knowing that Montreal, which we had never been to before, was only two hours away, we got to thinking... let's do Montreal!

So we Googled things to do in Montreal, saw that Don Henley was playing there on September 14th, and picked that date for the service. Yep, the date of Aunt Helen's funeral was determined by the Henley concert. She was always a huge Eagles fan.

We honored Helen with a very nice service at the Presbyterian Church in Saranac Lake. If you are an Eagles/Don Henley fan, our closing paragraphs from that piece on our dearly departed 94-year-old Aunt Helen might be your favorite ones we've ever written.

During Helen's service, not that we are looking ahead to the Henley concert, but as we reflect back upon the earlier times in Helen's life we realize that "The Heart of the Matter" is that before "The End of the Innocence" changed in a "New York Minute", and "All She Wants to Do is Dance" with "The Boys of Summer", the result was that her "Dirty Laundry" included "Leather and Lace."

But, "I Can't Tell You Why" with "The Long Run" for Helen "Already Gone" with a "Peaceful Easy Feeling", we are not going to "Take it Easy". We are going to check into the "Hotel California", have "One of These Nights", order another "Tequila Sunrise", "Take it to the Limit" and live "Life in the Fast Lane."

EPILOG TO THE PROLOGUE ~ So there's a sampling of our style. With a tendency toward the irreverent, we are going to tackle the Manson topic with a fresh approach. We have profoundly and purposefully peppered powerful poetry perpetuating the potential of every chapter with the goal of professing a story with the perfect balance of information and entertainment. When you finish our chronicle on this superbly sinister snapshot in American history you will walk away feeling like you know everything you need to know and have also enjoyed the sojourn to your destination.

As two former teachers we would like to jointly assume the role of that favorite teacher you had in high school. You remember the one. It was the teacher who was demanding that you work hard, but you didn't mind doing the work because the class was engaging and you knew you would emerge not only educated but inspired.

At this point please buckle your seat belts and, just like Sexy Sadie, prepare yourself to hear the rattling of the ice cubes in the cocktail shakers down in the canyon. Start Chapter 1 and join us for the chilling ride.

Oh, one final thing before we start. If anyone out there is looking to buy a half-week article on Lizzie Borden this is your lucky day!

Tim & Deb Smith
Mendon, New York
July 31, 2019

CHAPTER 1:
STORYLINE SAMPLER

The point could be made understandably
That murder sprees bypass insanity
But while killings dismay
What the hell can you say?
That's just part of the deal with the Family

MAGICAL MONTH ~ As we began writing this book in the beginning of 2019, there was a unique hat trick of 50th anniversaries looming on the horizon over the course of just a one-month period during that approaching summer. Yes, the sultry summer of '69 proved to be an eventful one. Within a month-long period of time, crazy things are happening all over the solar system. On July 20, Neil Armstrong becomes the first man to walk on the moon; on August 8-9 the Manson Family commits the Tate-LaBianca murders in Los Angeles, California; and on August 15-18 the Woodstock Music Festival takes place in Bethel, New York.

How's that for a manic month? And just for good measure, it also turned out to be the month we met. So on our own personal level we got to change "hat trick of anniversaries" to "grand slam of anniversaries". But in this book, we're going to focus in on just one anniversary, that being the Manson murders, and we're here to tell you one titillating and tempestuous tale. Let's get started.

The night of August 8, 1969 looms quietly hot and humid in the Los Angeles suburb of Bel Air. As they stealthily drop over the mansion's protective embankment onto the lawn of the home of actress Sharon Tate, one of the soon-to-be murderesses is struck by the silence, and perhaps the enigmatic enormity of the crime her crazed crew is about to commit.

Later, Susan Atkins aka "Sexy Sadie" will remember the moment, in her typically anti-establishment tone, and describe it as such. "It was so quiet," Sadie said, "you could almost hear the sound of ice rattling in cocktail shakers in the homes way down in the canyon."[1] Amongst the Family, it was well known that Sexy Sadie was one cynically sassy sister.

By the time Sexy Sadie and her three Family accomplices would leave the compound, five people would be dead. They would add to their death toll the following night and that all becomes part of the brazen debauchery detailed in this book. But brace yourself. We're going to employ a variety of methods and techniques the likes of which you have never before experienced.

Our goal in writing this book was not to have it be the definitive reference book on this topic. You can find that elsewhere. Our foremost goal was to have it be an engagingly entertaining read and, to that end, our strategy has been to strike the right balance between thoroughness and entertainment. If we found our research on a certain part of the trial to be boring, we chose not to pass that boredom onto you. We'll tell you what you need to know and move on quickly to the good stuff.

We've immersed ourselves in the action and aren't afraid to play with it – no matter how serious or somber the subject. This impish anti-establishment flavor is appropriate – if not expected – for the era about which we write. Regarding our book, a comment that was shared with us by our publisher was that he assessed our style as being a combination of Ken Kesey and Hunter Thompson. He added, "People who don't understand that era might not appreciate [the style], but the many who do understand it will be relieved to see someone else gets it (and them)."

For your entertainment pleasure, we've written some songs, limericks and poems. We're a bit irreverent, but we're thinking if you don't trend toward that persuasion a bit yourself, you probably wouldn't have picked this book up in the first place. About this aspect an English teacher we used to work with wrote, "I love the poems/limericks/songs… they are just the right hint of humor to pull off the black comedy genre."

Another critic wrote, "The limericks are an absolutely brilliant use of a transition technique."

So what else do we have in store for you? We're going to take this first chapter and turn it into what you might call our "Smith Sampler." One bodacious bonus we offer is that we'll provide you with step-by-step instructions on how to orchestrate an orgy, should you be put in charge of one. How's that for the ultimate combination of fun and practicality?!

We start with the Charles Manson playbook on orgy orchestration and then put our own whimsical spin on things. Since the time Charlie choreographed his last orgy technological advances have been made, but when you get to the bottom of things it still comes down to the people. Charlie felt that the key to a successful orgy was that the participants have their heads in the right place, and at this point we mean figuratively not literally. We'll get to that other part later.

A thought that occurs to us as we compose this introduction is how do we hook the hardcores? Well, even if you think you pretty much know this story already, we've got some hazy and unheard hallucinogenic highs in store for you. We've got books you've probably never read, sinister celebrity assassinations, and oh yeah… did you ever see the video from when an ABC techie kept his camera running for several minutes, unbeknownst to Manson, after the conclusion of a Diane Sawyer 20/20 interview? The footage is unbelievable, and to these treasures only we have the key. The good news is that we are more than willing to share.

Unless you're one of the few people who bought and read Susan Atkins/Sexy Sadie's 1977 book *Child of Satan, Child of God*, we will share with you something you never knew before. In our years of research on this book, there was no other place where we found the story she shares about the angry private conversation she alone overheard between Charles Manson and Tex Watson after Tex and his crew returned home from the Tate murders on the evening of August 8, 1969.

Did you ever hear about the Manson celebrity hit list? There were actually graphic plans in place regarding how they were going to murder Elizabeth Taylor, Richard Burton, Frank Sinatra, Tom Jones and Steve McQueen. We'll share the demonic details.

What if you're a sports fan? How can we change your life? This introduction can't go on forever, so we'll just choose one example. If we had to select just one team that might encompass the broadest spectrum of fans, the New York Yankees would certainly be a logical choice. Okay here's how life will never be the same again for all you fans of the Yanks. Picture the conclusion you're longing for every time you hear the umpire bark out, "Play ball!" at the beginning of the game.

If the Yankees win, the dugout will completely empty onto the infield grass, and perfunctorily form the double lines which will parade by each other facilitating the opportunity for the obligatory fist bumps, all occurring while players and coaches are marching to the tune of Frank Sinatra singing "New York, New York". After reading our book, you'll never be able to witness that scene again without a nauseatingly nagging thought burdening your brain. You can't help but feel the yearning for something you long for, but know you can never have. You're burdened by the knowledge that had the Manson Family succeeded in carrying out their full intentions, you might be the proud owner of a coin purse fashioned from the epidermis of Frank Sinatra made by the Mansons after they skinned him alive… with "That's Life" playing in the background.

Do you know what actually creates the most positive moment in the case for Charles Manson? Why it's the slick shtick of Tricky Dick Nixon! That tantalizing tale will begin to titillate in Chapter 16.

Charles Manson wrote songs with Dennis Wilson of the Beach Boys and also recorded an album at the group's studio. We'll tell you what Charles Manson song the Beach Boys recorded and released on both a single and an album. If you're old enough you might even remember watching the group perform it live on the Mike Douglas Show in 1969.

While it's Manson's connection with the Beach Boys that leads to his greatest musical success, the Beatles are the group by whom he is most fascinated. The one element of this book which might in turn fascinate you the most is the ability Manson had to manipulate the lyrics of the Beatles into validating the prophecies he was espousing. And the degree to which the Beatles, obviously inadvertently, happened to write songs which propped up the planks in the Manson manifesto is mind-blowing.

Then Charlie's next move is to tie the whole package together with a biblical connection. His go-to Bible passage is the Book of Revelation, Chapter 9 and again, it's uncanny how those words, written over 2,000 years ago, seem to be describing Charlie's vision and the Beatles at the same time.

The aspect of this which we find humorous is that Charlie was never a voracious reader, and you wouldn't think the Bible would have made his Top 10 list. But Charlie decides to give the Bible a chance because obviously if he can draw some parallels between the book of God and the book of Manson it would serve as the ultimate validation. How ironic is it that he has to read all the way to the last damn chapter in the book before he finds something that clicks!

What was the one publication that most greatly contributed to Manson's success? We'll fill you in on the famous self-help book which was the cornerstone of Manson's philosophy and the key to his becoming a master of manipulation.

One compelling storyline we'll share with you is the shocking level of ineptitude displayed by the police during the investigation. One can't help but make a connection between this and the O.J. Simpson case. In the two most high-profile murder cases in the history of Los Angeles, the LAPD comes off like the Keystone Cops in an old Hollywood movie.

Here are a few highlights that you have to look forward to. After confidential inside police information is leaked to the press, a citizen calls LAPD to inform them that he had found the gun used in the murders and turned it into the LAPD six weeks ago. "Hey boys, you know that murder weapon you're looking for?... you already have it!"

The killers had discarded bloody clothes on their way home from the Tate murders as described in grand jury testimony. Several weeks after that testimony, a local TV news crew stages a reenactment based on that testimony, pulls over at the first logical spot, gazes down into the ravine and Voila!... there are the bloodstained clothes.

After nearly 10,000 man-hours of police work the case is cracked. So all that money invested in police overtime finally proved worth the investment, right? Nope. It was the dime that a jailhouse snitch put into a payphone to call the LAPD and tell them who did it... a fact that the department conveniently neglects to mention at the celebratory press conference.

We're going to tell you the highest Happy Meal story you've ever heard. Next time you hit the Golden Arches try the McAcid-burger. It's a seasonal sensation and available for a short time only.

We're going to close this chapter with a final teaser for you. One of the most endearing characters in our book is certainly Lotsapoppa. How did he get his name you ask? Well, he is a huge black dude noted for his sexual endowment and overactive libido. Lotsapoppa gets lotsapussy.

He would also serve as an asterisk to a go-to claim that Charles Manson would often make later in his life. Always maintaining his innocence Manson would routinely boast, "I never killed nobody." While that may have been true, there was a point in his life that Manson was sure he had killed someone.

Manson and Lotsapoppa get into a dispute over drug money. Manson ends up shooting him in the belly and in an attempt to save his life, Lotsapoppa pretends like he's Lotsa-dead. Upon his subsequent release from the hospital, Lotsapoppa has his friends confirm his "death" to Manson in order to prevent Charlie from returning to take a second shot at it.

Imagine the frivolity that will ensue when Charlie and the big man later cross paths in an L.A. courthouse and Charlie finds himself face-to-face with a ghastly ghost from his ghoulish past. Son of a bitch if it's not Lotsapoppa! This is one reunion you will not want to miss.

So climb on board and let the games begin. Trust us... there's never a dull moment in Mansonland.

The chicks seem to dig Lotsapoppa
The dude was the big enchilada
But things hit rock bottom
And then Manson shot him
Which made Chuck persona non grata

CHAPTER 2:
MOMMIE DEAREST, THE EARLY YEARS
(1934-1967)

OPENING ACT ⁓ Charles Miles Manson is born on November 12, 1934, to Kathleen Maddox, a hard-drinking sixteen-year old prostitute. When Manson's biological father finds out that Kathleen is pregnant, he leaves her and she ends up marrying Eugene Manson before Charles is born. Eugene sticks around just long enough to provide Charles with a surname before bolting. Charles Manson never even sees his biological father and his last name comes from a man to whom he is not related. Talk about your rough starts.

On August 1, 1939, Manson's mother and her brother Luther rob a gas station, knocking out the attendant with Coke bottles. If you're old enough, you may remember those heavy old returnable Coke bottles, tinted a translucent green, and built solidly enough to withstand being recycled hundreds of times. Unless of course if you smash it to pieces by cracking it over the top of someone's skull while committing a robbery.

Probably no big surprise since we're obviously not watching master criminals at work here but, soon after the heist, the criminal team is caught. Manson's "Mommie Dearest" is dealt a five-year prison sentence. During this time Manson is passed around amongst relatives until his mother is paroled in 1942, and at that point the family of two moves to Charleston, West Virginia. Take me home, country roads.

REFORM SCHOOLS ⁓ During the next five years Kathleen Manson is in and out of several things; including jail, relationships, and rehab. Charles is displaying an increasing array of antisocial behaviors, primarily burglaries. In 1947 his mother, feeling she can no longer handle the 12-year-old Charles, sends him to Gibault School for Boys, a reform school run by Catholic priests in Terre Haute, Indiana.

In 1948 he runs away from Gibault and embarks upon a series of car thefts, gun thefts and armed robberies which land him in the Indiana Boys School. After escaping from this institution, he steals a car and heads west, robbing several gas stations along the way. Manson is eventually arrested in Utah, and since driving a stolen car across state lines is a federal crime, he is sent to an even more rigid institution, Washington D.C.'s National Training School for Boys. Aptitude tests given him upon admission indicate that while he is illiterate, he has an above average IQ.

RELEASE, MARRIAGE, REINCARCERATION - Manson moves through a series of institutions before finally being released in May 1954. In January 1955, he marries a hospital waitress named Rosalie Jean Willis. In October, three months after he and his pregnant wife have arrived in Los Angeles, he is again charged with car theft and is in jail for the birth of his son Charles Manson Jr.

Here's the first time in this book where we're going to go a bit sideways. Please allow us to offer up this hypothetical homeroom first-day-of-school scenario. Knowing you are Manson's son you obviously enter the building with a bit of social skepticism about school. Upon proceeding to your first room assignment, the homeroom teacher begins to call out names to alphabetically arrange students in a seating chart which will most efficiently facilitate an accurate attendance assessment on a daily basis.

You, as well as your fellow classmates, are perfunctorily patient during the initial phases of this process, but nerves kick in and you feel your lower back growing moist with sweat as the teacher nears the middle of the alphabet. Every name called out before yours has prompted minimal response from the other students. Sure, when the teacher calls out the names of the hot chicks it prompts the guys in class to perhaps steal a quick glance.

But you know the most monumentally memorable moment of the roll call is going to be all yours. When the seats are assigned and the class is informed that occupying the back seat in row two will be "Charles Manson Jr." it becomes an all-eyes-on-you spectacle, unlike any other.

That first day of school's quite peculiar
You never suspect the words you'll hear
Assigned In row two
Sitting right next to you
Is none other than Charles Manson Jr.

Despite changing his name, Charlie Jr. is apparently unable to escape the psychological shackles of his heritage. He commits suicide in 1993.

BACK ON THE STREETS & THE HONEYMOON HAREM ~
Paroled in September of 1958, Charles Manson is back on the streets by November, with pimping as his primary source of income. Feeling the need to branch out and diversify the spectrum of his criminology, Charlie expands into the formidably friendly field of check fraud. Within a year of his release, in September of 1959, he pleads guilty to a charge of having falsely cashed a U.S. Treasury check.

We share next what would probably qualify as a breakdown in our court system. Manson ends up receiving a charge of only probation and a 10-year suspended sentence. How does Charlie pull this one off? Manson has one of his prostitutes, Leona, go to court and deliver a pleafully powerful performance professing her deep love for him and her desire to marry Manson if he were free. The judge grants parole and by year's end the couple does marry.

Truth be told, there's not a lot of true romance in this story so no matter how shallow the opportunity is, let's seize the moment. We're not sure of the bridal gift stores at which the couple is registered, and details of the wedding reception are sketchy, but this much we do know. After marrying Leona, what follows is an historical Hollywood honeymoon hoe down. Those last two words of the previous sentence certainly qualify as one of our most appropriate puns ever.

As they head out for the honeymoon, Leona grabs a horny hooker gal pal and, looking to do some serious business, Charlie hauls the girls through Arizona to New Mexico in April. Rumor has it that during the Easter parade, prostitution is prevalent in Prescott, Arizona. Please proceed patiently. Once again, we are heartily hinting that this harrowing honeymoon is hardly made in Heaven.

GO DIRECTLY TO JAIL ~ Upon their eventual arrival in New Mexico, Charlie and the chicks are by no means presented with the key to the city of Albuquerque. They immediately plunge into prostitution and are quickly caught. Because they are from out of state, Manson is arrested for violation of the Mann Act (transporting women across state lines for the purpose of prostitution). After they are temporarily released, Manson correctly realizes that the pending investigation will turn up his California crimes so Charlie takes his shady show on the road to Texas.

Landing in Laredo, the trio turn tricks, and are once again caught up in a prostitution crackdown. This time the authorities are a little more thorough in their background check and the dots are connected between this crime and Manson's current probationary status in California. That probation is rescinded, subsequently leading to his next significant incarceration which is at the United States Penitentiary at McNeil Island, Washington.

> *Your honeymoon gig was a hoot*
> *Heading east through the desert your route*
> *Let's take them to Texas*
> *And hire out some sex thus*
> *Pimp your wife and her pal prostitute*

CHAPTER 3:
THE BEACH BOYS AND THE BEATLES
(MARCH-AUGUST, 1967)

1960'S ROCK MUSIC ~ One significant aspect of Charles Manson's Washington prison time would be that hearing the Beatles on the *Ed Sullivan Show* sparks a significant interest in music on his part. He is able to be given guitar lessons by a fellow inmate and begins to cultivate what is at least a modest talent in the musical field. He will later become a singer/songwriter on the fringe of the L.A. music scene, most notably collaborating with Dennis Wilson of the Beach Boys. More on that to follow.

But while we're on the subject of music, allow us to share the following urban legend with you. There was a longstanding rumor that Charles Manson had auditioned unsuccessfully for the Monkees during the 1965 tryouts for that hit TV show. However, if dates are cross referenced for the Monkees auditions with Manson's dates of incarceration (1961-67), it can be positively determined that Manson and the Monkees never crossed paths. But hey, before the days of the internet, when Google wasn't only a few keystrokes away, it was easier to pull off such a hoax.

Meanwhile, let's shift from late 1960's rock, back to the maniacal Manson story. On March 21, 1967, after having spent more than half of his 32 years in prisons and other institutions, Manson is released.

BACK ON THE STREETS #2 ~ It should be noted that while serving his time at McNeil Island, in addition to working on his musical abilities, Manson also seriously pursues another objective. He takes advantage of opportunities afforded him and hones his reading and writing skills, significantly contributing to his ability to influence others when he gets out. The following fact could be perhaps perceived ironically, but the book Manson reads in prison which most helps formulate his futuristic philosophy is Dale Carnegie's *How to Win Friends and Influence People*. Makes sense, doesn't it?

Detailing circumstances that might now seem bizarre, prior to his release, Manson pleads with prison officials to allow him to stay. He has spent most of his life in jail, it's where he is most comfortable, and he is concerned with what might happen should he be allowed to reenter society.

Maybe somebody should have listened to him. For legal reasons that perhaps should be changed, if they haven't already, the State of California is unable to comply. That being said, despite his requests to the contrary, Manson is released. Let the games begin.

"IF YOU'RE GOING TO SAN FRANCISCO - Be sure to wear some flowers in your hair" (Scott MacKenzie, 1967). So, you're in California; it's the late '60's and if some sex and drugs and rock and roll are right up your alley, you would head straight for the Haight-Ashbury section of San Francisco. If somebody had done the roll call there, within two days of Manson's release, Charlie would have answered, "Here."

Revisiting some of the pros and cons of Manson's upbringing, while he bears the scars from a horrific early family life, he is extremely charismatic and people are drawn to him. Within months of his arrival, he begins to attract a cult of followers which will come to be known as the Manson Family. The Family demographics trend highly toward the female persuasion. Manson is masterful in his ability to manipulate women.

In terms of playing his cards right, San Francisco is the perfect location for him to form his cult, and L.A. will be the perfect location for the culmination. More on L.A. later. During this timeframe, the city of San Francisco is establishing itself as the hub of the counterculture hippie movement. As Manson begins to form his Family, this might have been the hypothetical questionnaire.

QUINTESSENTIAL QUIZ - Please check all of the following boxes in which you are interested:

❑ Sex ❑ The Beatles
❑ Music ❑ Experimental Drugs

If you have checked three or more of the previous boxes please show up at the Manson Family meeting at Haight-Ashbury. Hey, if we were there, we might have signed on.

Impeccable timing has Charles Manson arriving in San Francisco right at the beginning of 1967's Summer of Love and quickly establishing himself as a hippie guru capable of recruiting a cult following. While, as we said, he primarily procures women, he calculatingly adds a few select men who are strong enough to do the heavy lifting when that is required.

At this point it's clearly time for a field trip. In a move that would basically be copied by the Partridge Family a year later, the Manson Family buys a used bus, takes out most of the seats, paints it in psychedelic colors and hits the road. Contrary to the Partridge Family, the Manson Family has no hit singles before painting their bus and cruising California. The Family travels as far north as Washington, and as far south as Mexico, finally landing in Los Angeles, the City of Angels. Oh, the irony of it all.

Of course, the real inspiration for the Manson bus stemmed from the exploits of Ken Kesey and the Merry Pranksters, the crew sometimes credited with initiating the hippie movement. Beginning in 1964, the Pranksters merrily toured the country in their psychedelic painted school bus named Furthur. They were known for their experimentation with LSD and connections with the early Grateful Dead. Once you finish reading our book may we suggest Thomas Wolfe's *The Electric Kool-Aid Acid Test*, the definitive telling of the Kesey tale.

There once was a Beach Boy named Dennis
Who lived in a beach house in Venice
Surf's Up, California
But Dennis we warn ya
Those hippie chicks can be a menace

DENNIS WILSON - While Manson is obsessed with the Beatles, he actually attains success on the fringe of the L.A. rock scene through his connection with the Beach Boys. This connection begins when the Beach

Boys' drummer Dennis Wilson picks up the exact same pair of hitchhiking Manson girls for the second time.

Feeling like the second consecutive pick-up seems to be more than fate, Dennis brings them back to his Pacific Palisades home. In the post-sex conversation banter, Dennis mentions the Beach Boys involvement with Maharishi Mahesh Yogi. Charlie's girls respond by revealing that they have their own guru. Small world, isn't it?

This facilitates a meeting between Dennis Wilson and Charles Manson where their mutual interest in sex, drugs and rock & roll proves to be the foundation for a friendship, as well as a musical collaboration. Dennis proceeds to introduce Manson to some of his associates in the music world. "This is Charlie," Wilson tells friends. "He is the wizard, man. He is a gas."[1]

It is in a related situation when Manson becomes familiarized with the house where the Sharon Tate murders will eventually occur. On one occasion Wilson takes Manson to that house, at 10050 Cielo Drive, to meet record producer Terry Melcher and his girlfriend Candice Bergen who currently live in the house which will later become the residence of Roman Polanski and Sharon Tate.

Another irony in this thread of the storyline, is that Charles "Tex" Watson, who will eventually become the actual hit man at the Tate-LaBianca murders, meets Manson for the first time at Dennis Wilson's house. This almost surrealistic scenario surfaces when Dennis has an automobile accident and has to hitchhike home.

That storyline, in and of itself, gives us pause to reflect upon societal changes that have occurred in our lifetime. Think about it... you're one of the most famous and wealthy rock stars on the planet, and you're actually hitchhiking? But what are your options? It's not like you can fast forward to the future and find your cell phone. Hell, at that period in time you couldn't even fast forward an audio tape.

Subsequently, Dennis Wilson is in a surf's-down situation, stranded in Santa Monica, on the road with his thumb out, hoping for a helpful hippie to pull over and whisk him back to Pacific Palisades. What in the world are the odds? Of all the people who might pull over, he is picked up by a then naïve kid from Texas named Charles Watson. Upon driving

Dennis back home, young Watson encounters a scene unlike any he has ever experienced before.

WHERE THE GIRLS ARE ~ This shit never happens in Texas. When the two men get back to Wilson's home in Pacific Palisades the place is filled with Manson girls. Watson is given his choice of the girls there as a reward for his kind act of bringing Dennis back home, and finds himself feeling like a mosquito in a nudist colony; he doesn't know where to start. Ultimately, Manson comes to the determination that Watson is a man who has the potential to productively perform a function fundamentally facilitating the Family's funfest. Tex Watson joins the Manson Family that day. His life will never be the same again. Remember his name. Wilson's advice to Watson at this point might have been...

Your kindness allows you to pick one
Feel free to just climb on and lick one
But while they may please you
They, too, can disease you
Be careful and don't choose a sick one

When you compress all the Dennis Wilson/Charles Manson connections into one compost, the culmination of the combination is a crazily compelling conglomerate of coincidences. Allow us to review. The relationship begins when Dennis, who often picks up hitchhikers, picks up the same two Manson girls two days in a row, prompting the predictable sexual threesome. Manson subsequently stops in, bringing the incumbent bevy of babes for a Beach Boy bonanza.

During this honeymoon period, Wilson takes Manson to the home of record producer Terry Melcher, inadvertently allowing Manson to case the site of the future home of Sharon Tate, the home in which she will be murdered. Only days later Dennis Wilson has an automobile accident, and doesn't the hitchhiking thread kick in once again!

While hitching a ride, Dennis is picked up by none other than Charles "Tex" Watson, who will drive Dennis home, meet Charles Manson, and get to have sex with the first Manson girl of his choice. Watson subsequently joins the Family and one year later will assume the leadership role in the assassination team that Charles Manson will send to the home of Sharon Tate.

It is an acknowledged fact that Charles Manson participated in recording sessions with the Beach Boys. Beach Boys engineer Stephen Desper confirms this by saying, "Once the concept of Manson trusting an expert was established, he did fairly well as an artist and things moved along. He settled into the whole recording scene and we did get some good tracks." In Charles Manson's autobiography he wrote, "I was at (Dennis Wilson's brother) Brian Wilson's studio and we did a pretty fair session, putting down about ten songs."[2]

Music historian Andrew Doe has the following comment about these songs which were recorded with the backing of a small orchestra. Let it be said that neither Brian Wilson's appreciation of, nor participation in, this session should be assumed. Doe summarized this situation by saying, "These recordings seeing an official release have not a hope in hell."[3]

One of the songs Charles Manson and Dennis Wilson collaborate on is called "Cease to Exist". After parting with Manson, Dennis revises and retitles the song as "Never Learn Not to Love" and it is released as the B-side of the group's "Bluebirds Over the Mountain" single in 1968 and included on the Beach Boys 20/20 album which came out in 1969.

DENNIS ENDS THE RUN OF "FUN FUN FUN" ~ Of the Beach Boys, Dennis Wilson has always been the party boy, but even Dennis has his breaking point. While hosting a cult dominated by females dedicated to the concept of free love, certainly has its advantages, but it can also be a misnomer. When the tab for paying all the expenses exceeds $100,000, Wilson decides to cut his losses and evict the Manson menagerie. After all, Dennis has always been pretty good about picking up chicks on his own. About the experience Dennis would later say, "I'm the luckiest guy in the world, because I got off only losing my money."[4]

> *Chuck, I'm having my personal lawyers*
> *Rid my house of your trespassing followers*
> *Your girls can still blow me*
> *But actually you owe me*
> *Thousands and thousands of dollars*

CHAPTER 4:
THE WHITE ALBUM GOES HELTER SKELTER
(SEPTEMBER-DECEMBER, 1968)

SPAHN RANCH ~ After being kicked out of Dennis Wilson's house, Manson next establishes a base for the Family at Spahn's Movie Ranch which is located in the Simi Hills northwest of Los Angeles. This ranch is an eerie spot which strangely befits the fact that it would eventually become the launching pad for hippie cult death squads to foray into L.A. to commit mass murders in the hope of inciting the race war prophesized by their leader.

The Spahn Ranch had been a former set for TV and movie productions so it was built as an old cinematographically stereotypical Western town with the building facades recreating the businesses one would expect to see in an old movie or television show. There is a sheriff's office, blacksmith shop, post office, saloons, etc. Each side of the street has a covered boardwalk running the combined length of all the buildings. Those are the old west equivalent of sidewalks, just like you'd see in the movies.

But by the late 1960's, Spahn Ranch's marquee Main Street buildings have deteriorated to the point where no more movies or TV shows are being filmed there. The ranch is still owned by George Spahn, a nearly blind 80-year-old man whose primary source of income has dwindled down to the sale of tourist pony trail rides around his historic but decaying facility.

As we assess this situation, it provides a brilliant example of Charles Manson becoming the master manipulator and deftly displaying his ability to orchestrate the circumstances to which he's been availed in order to have them work for his greatest benefit. George Spahn, owner of the ranch, is low on funds, owns a lot of property and needs help with the upkeep. Subsequently, charming Charlie swoops in like a voracious vulture anticipating the quick kill.

Here's the proposed deal for George. In return for the use of multiple old buildings to house his Family, "Charlie's Angels" will do all the work necessary to maintain the facility, and also serve as George's "seeing-eye dogs", helping him navigate his property. Understandably skeptical, Spahn is reticently reluctant to have his personal property descended upon by some type of cult but, as is his forté, Manson manages to manipulate Spahn by playing to his manhood.

As this episode of *Let's Make a Deal* plays out, when the clause is included that Spahn will be provided with sex on a regular basis by Lynette Fromme, one of Charlie's chicks, the deal is sealed. Included herein is the greatest nickname story in Manson Family lore. One of Charlie's go-to psychological strategies is to assign nicknames to his cult members, which serves the dual purpose of enhancing their connection to the Family, while distancing connections to their past.

Other than "Sexy Sadie", the Manson Family nickname that certainly resonates the most throughout history is one not bestowed by Charlie himself. Lynette Fromme's nickname became "Squeaky" bestowed upon her by the 80-year-old George because of the sounds she makes while they are having sex.

Spahn may have been blind, but the man knew how to drive a stiff deal. If the name Squeaky Fromme rings a bell for you, there's a reason why. Lynette "Squeaky" Fromme is the Manson Family member who attempts to assassinate President Gerald Ford in 1975.

> *He's 80, and Squeaky's 19*
> *Yet upon his jeans she would cream*
> *She'd say, George, be patient*
> *I know that you're ancient*
> *But ain't I a ranch owner's dream?*

DEATH VALLEY ~ In addition to their primary location at the Spahn Ranch, it is decided that the Manson Family should also arrange for additional accommodations in Death Valley. The Death Valley digs provide an escape for the times the Family might want to avoid the attention incumbent with living in L.A. Also, the ranch is in closer proximity to the underground cave in which the Family plans to hide to escape the impending apocalypse. More on that later.

On October 31, an advanced-mission crew of Manson Family members heads toward Death Valley with two leads, which both pan out. On November 1, the mission is successful in securing the use of the abandoned Myers Ranch which is owned by the grandmother of a Manson Family member.

Looking to expand their options, the Manson entourage next approaches the nearby little-used ranch of an old woman known to them only as Ma Barker. While introducing themselves as a musical act, Manson establishes credibility by gifting her with a gold album awarded to the Beach Boys which had been given to him by Dennis Wilson.

He asks if she would be willing to exchange accommodations on her ranch for his Family performing handiwork and necessary repairs on her property. The Beach Boys gold album for the 1964 classic *The Beach Boys Today* subsequently changes hands for the second time. The chain of possession has passed from Dennis Wilson to Charles Manson to Ma Barker. Help me, Rhonda!

THE WHITE ALBUM ~ It is during December of 1968 that Manson becomes totally obsessed with the music of the Beatles, in particular *The White Album*, which has just been released. As we know, Manson does have some musical talent and expertise which he uses to enhance a thesis whereby the Beatles are predicting the same type of social upheaval that he is, and he seeks to connect with them.

Taking the whole concept one step higher, Manson even suggests that the Beatles are directing the Family to undertake the actions which will lead to them being the select group of white people to survive the impending apocalypse and ascend to their rightful positions as leaders of society.

Of course it all sounds crazy. But if you exam Manson's work on an analytical level it's actually rather impressive, in a twisted kind of way. He goes through multiple songs on *The White Album* and comes up with an interpretation of how each song is corroborating his preaching and prophecies.

And for the first time, Manson also bestows a name upon his futuristic philosophy. From this point on, thanks to the Beatles, Manson's collective predictions for the future will become known as "Helter Skelter". When we initially started to research this, we found it hard to believe that the whole notion of racial upheaval, somehow connected to the Beatles, was something anybody would consider buying into.

But in reading Manson's interpretations of Beatles lyrics, one can be fascinated by his ability to intertwine them with his own Helter Skelter philosophies. It becomes easy to see how, if someone were the kind of person who was prone to conspiracy theories or easily influenced, they might be vulnerable to Manson's manipulation.

Chapter 5:
The New Year's Eve Manifesto
(New Year's Eve, 1968)

NEW YEAR'S EVE ~ It's New Year's Eve 1968. On a cold winter's night, the Manson Family is hovered, around their campfire, in Death Valley and not watching the ball drop in Times Square. Instead they are listening to Charlie Manson's New Year's Rockin' Eve featuring the Beatles. Apparently, Dick Clark, who will start his *New Year's Rockin' Eve* tradition in 1972, is not available. As the group warms itself around the fire, they are about to have imparted upon them the Manson manifesto. We'll call it the New Year's Eve rollout.

On this festive evening, Manson has gathered his congregation together for a landmark sermon. Obviously, there are no handheld recording devices in the audience that night, but if you could somehow go back in time and retrieve any single audio from the annals of human history, this would certainly be one to rank high on the list.

As his cult huddles around him in the desert, the Family lights a holiday bonfire. In the glow of devilishly dancing flames, Manson prophesizes that 1969 will be the year of Helter Skelter. This will be the year that the ball is going to drop, so to speak.

In our total researching and analysis of the Charles Manson story and his ability to so manipulate and control the behavior of his followers, herein lies the centerpiece. Manson is able to take a basically convoluted and skewed story and sell it to a Family of disciples through an enlighteningly empowered existentialism. He is able to take existing lyrics from the Beatles and verses from the Bible and manage to craftily create a scenario where he can attribute an interpretation of those words to advocate his self-fulfilling prophesies.

To that end, if you're of the anti-establishment ilk, exhilarated by the espousal of existential theories, climb aboard our bandwagon because we are about to direct you toward a complete understanding of the Manson mission, as maniacally misconceived as it may have been.

TURBULENT TIMES ~ The tumultuous events of 1968 certainly contribute to the salability of Manson's theory. Okay, let's do the year in review. In 1968, the war is raging in Vietnam. A divided nation is justifiably debating the wisdom of so many lives being lost in what would become the first war the United States ever lost. On April 4, Martin Luther King Jr. is assassinated. On June 5, Robert F. Kennedy is assassinated. Preaching the apocalypse has never been easier.

It would be at the 1968 New Year's Eve sermon that Manson would share with the entire congregation, for the first time, the theories he has been working on whereby the Beatles have been speaking cryptically to the Family and subscribing to the same apocalyptic vision. The Manson Family New Year's Eve party welcomes in 1969 with a sense of anticipation, knowing that the launch of Helter Skelter is imminent.

What is Helter Skelter? Here's the explanation of Charles Manson's theory. The upheaval of Helter Skelter will begin with the ghastly murders of whites by blacks. The white victims will be affluent, upscale, establishment folks; the type of people that the anti-establishment Manson Family refers to as "Pigs" or "Piggies". The murders of these high society white folks will certainly lead to a white retaliation.

The white crusade into the ghettos to extract revenge will prompt an angry response from "blackie", which is the singular term Manson uses in his lexicon to collectively refer to all black people in general. The retribution of blackie will lead to an all out racial civil war. Contributing to the chaos will be the developing rift between those whites who have compassion for the blacks and those who do not. That infighting amongst the whites will weaken their race to the point where blackie will emerge victorious, thus eliminating the whites from our society.

The only exception to the white annihilation will be the Manson Family, who will have avoided the Caucasian apocalypse while hiding out in their cave below Death Valley. Then, as Charlie hypothesizes, blackie will be too inexperienced and incompetent to govern themselves, thus enabling the Manson Family to ride in on their white horses and come to the rescue. Relieved to welcome back their former oppressors, blackie can now breathe a collective sigh of relief, grateful that they once again have white people to run their lives. Hmmm… we just can't see what could possibly go wrong with this plan.

We are going to save the bulk of "The Beatles and the Bible" thread for Bonus Chapter 1, because, as you'll see, that component of the story can fill volumes on its own. (N.B.: Bonus Chapters are only available in the print version of this book.) Much of the vision of imminent apocalypse Charles Manson has personally fashioned is based upon his interpretation of the Bible's "Revelation Chapter 9". The fact that *The Beatles* (a.k.a. *The White Album*), released in November 1968, includes a song titled "Revolution #9" is a cornerstone to Manson's preaching. As we will share in the next chapter the Beatles have inadvertently dropped a gigantic gift right into Charlie's lap in terms of his ability to sell the theory that there is a genuine connection between the Beatles and the Family.

Again, we want to refer you to Bonus Chapter 1 in which we'll analyze the hell out of this, no pun intended. But coming up in Chapter 5, please savor our short list of sensations. The hottest of Charlie's chicks is Susan Atkins, an early member of the Family who Charlie has nicknamed Sadie. On *The White Album* there is a track called "Sexy Sadie". Let the game of coincidences begin.

> *In choosing the perfect disciple*
> *Choose wisely and you might be liable*
> *To take Charles Manson*
> *And give him a chance, son*
> *To link up the Beatles and Bible*

CHAPTER 6:
DISSECTING *THE WHITE ALBUM*
(DECEMBER 31, 1968-MARCH 23, 1970)

When Manson delivers his New Year's Eve speech where he fully explains his theory and the connection to the Beatles' lyrics they play *The White Album* over and over. But there are five songs in particular that Manson considers to be the centerpiece of the connection between his Family and the most popular rock band in the world. Right here we will share with you short summaries of the interpretations that Manson drew from these five songs. As we mentioned, if you would like to read more complete interpretations please go to our Bonus Chapter 1 called "The Beatles and the Bible."

BLACKBIRD ⁓ This track from *The White Album* plays right into Manson's hand for two reasons. It uses the word "rise" which is go-to terminology repeated by Charlie. That is one of the words written in blood on the wall at the LaBianca murders. And if you equate "blackbird" with the black race, then you have a clear interpretation of the blacks rising up to overtake the whites.

Lyrics include. "Blackbird singing in the dead of night/Take these broken wings and learn to fly/All your life/You were only waiting for this moment to arise." The final line in the song is, "Blackbird fly into the light of the dark black night."

HELTER SKELTER ⁓ This one has the added significance of serving as the title Charles Manson has bestowed upon his prophecy of the impending Armageddon resulting in the racial war that will turn the world upside down. When Manson addresses the Family on New Year's Eve 1968, he says, "Are you hep to what the Beatles are saying? Helter Skelter is coming down. The Beatles are telling it like it is."[1]

According to Manson, as has been stated, his followers will escape the violence of Helter Skelter by hiding out underground in Death

Valley. When the Beatles say "Look out/Helter Skelter/She's coming down fast/Yes she is," the implication is that the upcoming explosion of race-based violence is coming soon; Helter Skelter is imminent.

PIGGIES ⁓ In "Piggies" the piggies equal the establishment. Manson's favorite part of the song is verse 3 when the piggies are, "Living piggy lives/You can see them out for dinner/With their piggy wives/Clutching forks and knives/To eat their bacon."

The song goes on to say about the piggies that, "What they need's a damn good whacking." The interpretation of this one is pretty obvious. The establishment needs to get whacked. Regarding the cutlery mentioned in the song, it should also be noted that Leno LaBianca is left with a knife in his throat and a fork in his stomach.

REVOLUTION 1 ⁓ This one hinges on a single word which does not even appear on the lyric sheet included in the album. The chorus goes like this, "You say you want a revolution/Well you know we all want to change the world/But when you talk about destruction/don't you know that you can count me out (in)." Those two little letters "in" can effectively serve to change the entire meaning. While they do not appear in the lyric sheet, they are clearly audible.

Originally the lyrics advocate against violent protests but obviously the Beatles flip the whole meaning with the inclusion of that one additional final word. The "final word" the group seems to land on is "count me in" when it comes to the concept of violent revolution. To his captive New Year's Eve audience Manson proclaims that the Beatles are essentially saying, "Fuck this peace shit." In terms of his efforts to convince his followers that the Beatles are actually talking to them, this track is a gold mine.

REVOLUTION 9 ⁓ This was the track on *The White Album* that Manson deems to be the most significant, a comment that might seem surprising when it's noted that there are no true lyrics. The track is an audio collage of over eight minutes with psychedelic instrumentation and, best of all for Manson, some audible but muddled voices hidden beneath the surface. It's a cacophony of synthesizers, horns, drums and various other sounds including machine gun fire and the oinking of pigs. You can't sing along to this one.

More than any other song, you need to go to Bonus Chapter 1 to truly appreciate all of the connections Manson is able to draw from this track. The references are so numerous you can almost confirm how Manson was able to use them to so successfully suck his Family of kids into subscribing to his philosophy. Just to share a few of them with you here, Charlie points out spots where the muddled audio seems to include voices saying "lots of stab wounds" and "Charlie, Charlie, send us a telegram."

But the single most significant audio thread from this track is certainly the one Manson uses to connect the Beatles and the Bible in his prophecy. The degree to which the Beatles inadvertently prop up Charlie's preposterous predictions is profound. The title is the biggest thing. Through the garbled maze of sounds there is only one recurrent phrase. Periodically repeated, in a chant, are the words "Number 9, Number 9, Number 9." The Bible book and chapter which Manson uses as the centerpiece for his Helter Skelter theory is "Revelation 9."

Revelation 9, Revolution 9, Revelation 9, Revolution 9. The symmetry smashes you in the skull like you're being slugged with a sledgehammer. Revelation 9, Revolution 9, Revelation 9, Revolution 9.

The fact that Manson's biblical references were primarily based upon the Book of Revelation suggests a humorously unique reflection on our part. Charlie was never a voracious reader and you wouldn't think the Bible would be a go-to book for him. How ironic is it that the book in the Bible that clicks for him is literally the very last book?

You'd think that after the buzzkill of "Second Corinthians" he might have baled on the Bible. But not our Charlie; he felt that the Bible would have something in there for him somewhere and turns out he was right.

> *A race war of unknown duration*
> *where white folks face annihilation*
> *The summer will swelter*
> *Bring on Helter Skelter*
> *It's all in the book "Revelation"*

As we stated was the case with our Beatles song imagery, you need to go to Bonus Chapter 1 "The Beatles and the Bible" for the whole story. The same can be said for the Bible imagery. If you want the whole Garden of Eden you need to go to the back of the book. Presented here is a shortened summary.

In the Book of Revelation, the apostle says that he initially sees four angels and then another angel ascending. The interpretation of this is that the four angels are the Beatles and the other angel is Manson. There is a line about the fifth angel being given a key to the "bottomless pit." In Manson's interpretation, the bottomless pit equals the underground cave to which his Family will retreat to escape the apocalypse of Helter Skelter.

The angels are told not to hurt the men who have the seal of God on their foreheads. This foreshadows Manson and the Family cutting crosses into their foreheads during the trial. There are references to locusts who have hair like women. Locusts are literally a type of beetle, and the "hair like women" line is interpreted as a reference to the Beatles' long hair.

Out of the mouths of the locusts emanates "fire and smoke and brimstone" which is interpreted as acknowledging the power and popularity of the Beatles music. Finally "Revelation 9" goes on to say that the fire and brimstone will kill mankind, or to put it in the words of both the Beatles and Manson, "Helter Skelter." Again this is just a cursory overview but it does give a feel for the connectivity which Manson creates between the Beatles and the Bible. Amen.

YELLOW SUBMARINE ~ Perhaps prompted by the chilly temperatures on the night of his New Year's Eve address, Manson decides that the Family needs some warmer digs for the winter, so he seeks out a site in the city. On January 10, Manson sends word to the Family that he has found suitable accommodations for them. It is a huge canary yellow house on Gresham Street in the Canoga Park neighborhood of the San Fernando Valley region of L.A.[2] In Charlie's words it is a place where they can "be submerged beneath the awareness of the outside world."[3]

Because of the bright yellow color and the Beatles motif Manson has adopted for the Family, their new abode is given the moniker of the

"Yellow Submarine." Right now we're picturing the Family gathered around the fireplace with Charlie leading the gang in a raucous chorus of, "We all live in a yellow submarine, yellow submarine, yellow submarine."

Their hippie drug lifestyle was mellow
They lived in a submarine yellow
They lauded their evils
And just like the Beatles
Their mushrooms were not portabello

MANSON AND MELCHER ~ In February of 1969 Manson conceives the final portion of his plan. The Manson Family will record their own album which will mirror the coded messages of the Beatles' *White Album*. The Manson album will convey the Family's responses to the questions which the Beatles have posed for the Family on *The White Album*. At this point, Charles Manson has convinced his growing cult of the connectivity between the messages of the Beatles, the Bible and Charles Manson.

Confident that Charlie is pretty much spot on with his New Year's Eve predictions about the Helter Skelter future, the Manson Family pushes forward on the project to record their album. There is one person tangentially involved with this storyline who becomes particularly important at this point. That person would be Terry Melcher who is a successful record producer, as well as the son of Doris Day and the boyfriend of Candice Bergen.

Beach Boy Dennis Wilson had previously taken Manson to see Terry Melcher at 10050 Cielo Drive, the house that Sharon Tate is now living in. In addition to working with the Beach Boys, Terry Melcher's resumé also includes producing the Byrds, the Mamas & Papas, and Paul Revere & the Raiders. He was definitely a legend of the '60's.

Having met Melcher during the time he had spent with the Beach Boys, Manson decides to recruit him to produce the album he has envisioned for the Manson Family. Satisfied with the songs the Family has written and rehearsed, Manson contacts Melcher and arrangements are made for Melcher to stop by the Yellow Submarine on March 21, 1969, and hear the material. This is a major moment because Manson needs this domino to fall in place if Helter Skelter is to come to fruition.

To that end, Manson pulls out all the stops to get the house ready. The menu is to consist of salad, French bread, lasagna and homemade cookies. Charlie sets up all the musical equipment himself and directs the girls to clean up the house and roll some joints. Party preparations are properly in place, but for reasons unknown, Melcher fails to show.

Two days later, a snubbed Manson goes to the house where Melcher and Candice Bergen had lived when Manson met him. Unbeknownst to Manson, in February of that year, Melcher had moved out and the house is now occupied by film director Roman Polanski and his wife, actress Sharon Tate. Manson is informed by a photographer that Melcher no longer resides at this address.

As the photographer is attempting to explain to Manson the current situation at the house, Sharon Tate hears the voices from inside and walks out onto the porch. As the photographer explains that Manson's presence is the result of a mistake regarding a previous tenant, Sharon Tate and Charles Manson are standing about eight feet apart. While they never speak to each other, they certainly would have made eye contact.

Whether Manson already knows that this is a house which he might subsequently target, or the idea occurs to him while he is there, we'll never know. In yet another irony of this story, if Terry Melcher had showed up at the Manson house the day before, Sharon Tate might be alive today. On the occasion of the 50th anniversary of the murders she would have been 76 years old.

Ironically, Terry Melcher does subsequently visit the Spahn Ranch on at least two occasions to hear the Manson Family perform. Melcher however, never records the group which in retrospect is probably too bad. Obviously he isn't blown away by the material or he would have followed up.

A MERRY MANSON CHRISTMAS ~ But isn't it intriguing... the thought of hearing Charles Manson performing his songs surrounded by a bevy of female singers, some of whom are soon to become mass-murderesses. Our suggestion for the name of the group... The Manson

Tabernacle Choir. Surely their Christmas album would have been a killer.

Here's how we envisioned the lyrics for the first track which is Charlie's rewrite of "It's the Most Wonderful Time of the Year."

It's the most wonderful crime of the year
While Charlie's home chilling
His family's out killing, without any fear
It's the most wonderful crime of the year

It's the crap crappiest police force of all
Killers, they seize them
And then they release them, by dropping the ball
It's the crap, crappiest police force of all

There'll be warrants with wrong dates
And results that have fates
That actually hurt friends near and dear
It's the most wonderful crime of the year

If you find yourself hooked, the compete 12-track album is available exclusively for big fans of *The Beatles, The Bible & Manson* in our Tim & Deb's Superfan Kit #1 called *The Manson Family Christmas Album* at the end of the book. Have a Merry Manson Christmas and a Naughty New Year.

CHAPTER 7:
MURDER AND MAYHEM
(JULY 25-AUGUST 7, 1969)

GARY HINMAN ~ The unfortunate distinction of being the man who is the first person murdered by the Manson Family goes to one Gary Hinman. He is a music teacher who, by all accounts, is considered to be a kind and generous man. His generosity, however, proves to be his downfall. In step with the hippie vibe of the late '60's, Hinman occasionally provides a place to stay for some of the kids who subsequently join the Manson Family.

Upon hearing that Hinman has inherited a considerable amount of cash, (Susan Atkins sets the amount at $21,000 in her 1977 autobiography)[1], Manson sends a team to recruit Hinman into the Family. A successful induction will require that Hinman surrender his assets to the collective group.

Assigned to this mission are Bobby Beausoleil, Mary Brunner (by whom Manson has fathered a child), and Susan Atkins (aka Sexy Sadie). The recruitment does not go well. Informed of this, Manson stops by to contribute his power of persuasion. Apparently, however, having Manson slice off part of Hinman's ear with a sword is not the game changer Charlie hoped it might be.

At that point Charlie departs, leaving Beausoleil, Brunner and Atkins to hold Hinman hostage for another day. When it becomes apparent that there is no way this situation is going to end on a positive note, abiding by Manson's directions to be sure to take care of business, Beausoleil stabs Hinman to death.

What follows becomes a signature of the Manson murders. One benefit of stabbing deaths is that you always end up with so much blood on the floor that arts & crafts projects inevitably ensue. Artsy Susan Atkins uses the blood to paint a Black Panther paw on the wall and Beausoleil adds the phrase "Political Piggy." The Black Panther imagery is included of course to enhance Manson's goal of stoking racial unrest. In our ongoing motif of limericks, here's how Hinman might have summed this up for Manson.

> *Your gal pal just took her brazier off*
> *In hopes that my money I'll clear off*
> *And just give it to you*
> *what the hell do you do?*
> *But go cut my damn fuckin' ear off*

SETTING THE WHEELS IN MOTION ⁓ Manson has proclaimed 1969 to be the year that Helter Skelter is going to go down, so there is an expectation amongst the Family that something will be happening soon. As the months of 1969 begin to trickle away, there may have been some rumblings about when this impending apocalypse is actually going to begin.

By June, Manson has begun to suggest to some members of his inner circle that since blackie seems incompetent of getting the racial ball rolling on their own, it might be incumbent upon the Family to fan the flames and initiate the violence that will bring about Helter Skelter. In mid-June, while Manson and Family member Paul Watkins are discussing Helter Skelter, Manson tells Watkins, "It looks like we're gonna have to show blackie how to do it."[2]

By August, Charles Manson has clearly come to the conclusion that it's time to let the lethal games begin. On the afternoon of August 8, 1969, he announces to the Family, "It's time for Helter Skelter."[3] Even in the macabre of Mansonland, it is a proclamation that would make the hair stand up on the back of your neck.

LET THE GAMES BEGIN ⁓ Here's how Tex Watson sets this part up. At his trial he testifies, "Charlie called me over behind a car and handed me a gun and knife. He said for me to take the gun and knife and go up to where Terry Melcher used to live. He said to kill everybody in the house as gruesome as I could. I believe he said something about movie stars living there."[4] Also assigned to the Tex task force are Family members Susan Atkins, Linda Kasabian, and Patricia Krenwinkel.

The women in the Manson hierarchy are for the most part left out of the planning and policy making phases of the operation. It's been ingrained in them to follow directions and of this they do a masterful job. Manson's only directions to them are, "Do what Tex says. Leave a sign. You girls know what I mean, something witchy."[5]

The word "witchy" was more a part of the American lexicon in that era. It basically meant spooky and an example of the word's use was reiterated when the Eagles song "Witchy Woman" went to #9 in August of 1972.[6]

As we approach the trial, the degree to which Manson is able to dominate and manipulate his followers will become a key component. Think about it; the prosecution is going to be charged with the responsibility of convincing a jury to unanimously convict Manson of seven murders which occur when he isn't even at any of the crime scenes. While this scenario certainly presents a challenge, Manson's dominance is indeed a factor.

Manson dictates the Family's every move. He tells them when to eat and where to eat. He tells them when to sleep, where to sleep and who to sleep with. At mealtime no one can be served until he is seated, he often preaches during meals and no one may interrupt or talk while he is speaking.

ORGIES ⁓ When they have orgies, Charlie is the choreographer. In case you may be planning an orgy of your own soon, please allow us to share with you the following strategies, assured in the knowledge that we've learned them from the master. As you must certainly know your guests well, begin by divvying out your drugs and alcohol in a carefully calculated manner.

This is how Charlie orchestrates an orgy. Upon reaching that magical moment when all of your guests seem to have their heads in the right place, and we're talking figuratively not literally at this point, you craftily coax your participants to take their clothes off. At this point the pressure shifts, because it's imminently incumbent upon you to assume the lead in forming the conga line.

Departing from our brother Charlie's guru guidebook to group orgasm, please allow us share one personal note. Before you form that living room conga line, make sure your shades have been drawn if you live within camera shot of any neighbors. As we learned the hard way, forgetting to do that can really come back to bite you in the ass. And for the record, that last expression is again being offered figuratively, at this point. The literal interpretation of that one is still a few gulps away.

As you lead your naked conga line snaking its way from the living room, through the dining room, then around the kitchen table we must empower you to make one decision on your own. Based upon the layout of your house, your next move is to lead your line to the largest most plushly carpeted room available. Granted, your focus may be a bit compromised at this point, but if the thought of adding something new to your "to do" list does occur to you, jot down "call Stanley Steamer."

Going back to the Gospel of Charlie, Chapter 69: Verse 69, your next direction is to have everyone lie down on the floor in totally random positions, wherever they choose. Then you instruct everyone to take 12 deep breaths and exhale each one slowly. This enables your participants to increase their oxygen level and blood flow as this party moves from the conga line to the cunnilingus line. If you happen to be reading this on computer, here's a challenge you can use to test the solidity of your circuitry. Highlight cunnilingus and hit the synonym button. If your computer doesn't automatically crash and go into shut down mode, you're ready to move on to the next chapter. At your own risk.

Fully appreciating the value of extended foreplay, let's all gradually slide back into the orgy and put you back in charge. Just to make sure you remember where we left off, everyone is laying naked on the floor, with no sexual contact having yet been made. The pressure now shifts back to you, the leader, but not to worry. Think of it this way. If you've convinced all these people to strip naked, dance in a conga line, and assume a position on the floor; where are they going at this point? The coat check girl has clearly left the building.

Your next directions are to have all of your party participants reach out and gently touch and rub against each other. You, the director of this epic orgy, arrange the actors' bodies, positions, combinations and climaxes. You simultaneously fulfill the fantasies of all your actors, as well as your own. You are Jesus inspiring misled disciples into dubious deeds of dedicated devotion.

At this point we're going to leave the details of how your orgy will climax to your own vivid imagination. The point we were trying to drive home when we started this was to establish the level of Charles Manson's control over his Family… Mission Accomplished!

While their practice of mass fornication
Was often a source of elation
Free Love comes with tabs
They found out that crabs
Are more than a kind of crustacean

CHARLIE'S ANGELS ~ Of the many women who are a part of the Manson Family, there are really only four you need to get a complete grip on in order to follow what will happen during the upcoming murders and trial. Here's a quick rundown and review.

PATRICIA KRENWINKEL ~ She was one of the earliest Manson Family members and one of the two girls picked up while hitchhiking by Beach Boys' drummer Dennis Wilson. As we covered earlier in the book, the Dennis Wilson ~ Charles Manson connection ended up playing a significant role in the storyline of this drama. If Dennis had not taken Charlie to 10050 Cielo Drive to visit Terry Melcher, that destination would have never been on Manson's radar as a possible target and Sharon Tate might be comfortably enjoying her senior years picking up lifetime achievement awards like that honorary Oscar she never had a chance to win.

How's this for a drastic transition? For a time Krenwinkel taught Catechism (Roman Catholic religious instruction) and wanted to become a nun. To that end she enrolled in Spring Hill College, a Jesuit institution in Alabama. But before completing even one semester, she moved back to Manhattan Beach, CA where she met Charles Manson in 1967. Krenwinkel was actually just the third girl to join the Family. At the time of the writing of this book, she was then the longest-incarcerated female inmate in the California Penal system.

SUSAN ATKINS ~ She joined the Family early, early enough to have been a participant on their opening bus trip dubbed the Magical Mystery Tour. Her nickname was Sadie which Manson adjusted to "Sexy Sadie" after a song by that name was included on the Beatles' *White Album*. She lived up to that billing. Of the many Manson chicks, she was generally considered to have the hottest body, an irony which Manson effectively used to his advantage in convincing the Family that the Beatles were reaching out to them.

She thought Manson was Jesus which inspired an extreme level of devotion on her part. That, in addition to the length of her tenure with the Family, was probably why Manson chose her to go on the murder sprees. She was the most prolific of Charlie's murderesses, having been involved in eight of the nine confirmed killings.

LESLIE VAN HOUTEN ~ She grew up in a middle-class church-going family in the Los Angeles suburb of Altadena. Her high school years however saw her gradually make the transition from homecoming queen to hippie. She went from being a prom gown princess to a Manson murderess.

Van Houten came on board with the Manson Family during the summer of 1968 joining them at Spahn Ranch. Her passion for sex and LSD was a one-two punch that made her one of Charlie's favorite angels. After all, every Family needs a homecoming queen.

LINDA KASABIAN ~ She was one of the later recruits to the Family, visiting Spahn Ranch for the first time with a friend in the fall of 1968. She suffered from having had a terrible relationship with her father and stepfather, and her husband abandoned her and their child, taking off for South America. Manson played upon her failed relationships with men to captivate her, and cultivate her allegiance.

Kasabian was unique among the women described here as she was the only one to be granted immunity from prosecution in return for her testimony. This opportunity was offered to her because she was at the site of both the Tate and LaBianca murders, so she was able to provide eye witness testimony. But the way the two scenarios played out, she did not personally kill anybody and, without Manson knowing, she actually sabotaged one of his murder attempts. More on that later. She perceived Manson to be "Christ-like."

MATTHEW 24: 23-26

[23]*At that time if anyone says to you, "Look, here is the Messiah!" or, "There he is!" do not believe it.*
[24]*For false messiahs and false prophets will appear and perform great signs and wonders to deceive, if possible, even the elect[the clergy].*
[25]*See, I have told you ahead of time.*
[26]*So if anyone tells you, "There he is, out in the wilderness," do not go out; or, "Here he is, in the inner rooms," do not believe it.*

CHAPTER 8:
THE TATE MURDERS
(AUGUST 8-9, 1969)

BEL AIR BOUND ~ Returning to the scene of the crime in 1969, Tex Watson and his entourage of Susan Atkins, Patricia Krenwinkel and Linda Kasabian pile into an old Ford and head toward 10050 Cielo Drive in Bel Air to carry out their orders. As previously stated, Manson's directions to Watson are to kill everyone as gruesomely as possible and the directions to the girls are to do exactly what Tex tells them to do.

The former Terry Melcher residence is now being rented by movie director Roman Polanski and his wife, actress Sharon Tate, most famous for her role in the 1967 movie *Valley of the Dolls*. There are a few aspects of this destination which combine to make it an attractive target. It is secluded, one hundred yards from the gate to the closest neighbor and one hundred feet from the gate to the house.[1] Being secluded, it is also vulnerable.

On this particular night, Polanski happens to be in Europe working on a film. But Sharon Tate is home and she has guests. Obviously, this is not going to be good news for the guests, but it is good news for Manson because it puts more high-profile targets at a single murder site. Tate's guests that night include famous hair stylist Jay Sebring, coffee magnate Abigail Folger and her boyfriend Voytek Frykowski.

Upon arrival at 10050 Cielo Drive, Tex Watson climbs the telephone pole, and cuts the phone line assuring that no outgoing calls can be made. Thinking the gate might be electrified or rigged with an alarm, they climb a brushy embankment to the right of the gate and drop onto the grounds.

WRONG PLACE-WRONG TIME ~ Just then, headlights approach them from farther within the property. Watson orders the women to hide in the bushes. In one of the most extreme examples ever of being in the wrong place, at the wrong time, eighteen-year old Steven Parent is leaving the estate's guest house just as the Manson crew is heading in.

Fearing that Parent might have seen them, Watson approaches the vehicle and orders the oncoming driver to halt. Watson then shoots him four times in the chest and abdomen killing him. Subsequently, Watson orders Kasabian to stay by the car and keep an eye on the gate while the other three head toward the Tate residence. As fate would have it, this directive to Kasabian turns out to be what would keep her out of jail for the rest of her life.

INSIDE THE HOUSE ~ By now it is after midnight and inside, the evening's proceedings are winding down. Watson is able to stealthily cut a window screen to gain entry and then go to the front door to let in Atkins and Krenwinkel. The first person they encounter is Frykowski who is sleeping on the couch in the living room. When Frykowski asks the intruders who they are and why they're here, Tex Watson kicks him in the head and says, "I'm the devil, and I'm here to do the devil's business."[2] Probably not the answer Frykowski is hoping for.

Watson sends Atkins and Krenwinkel to round up the other residents of the house and forces them into the living room. Watson throws a rope he's brought over one of the room's ceiling beams and ties the two ends around the necks of Sharon Tate and Jay Sebring. When Sebring complains about the rough treatment of the pregnant Tate, Watson shoots him.

Abigail Folger is forced back to a bedroom by Krenwinkel who steals $70 out of her purse. Krenwinkel ushers Folger back to the living room just in time to see Watson stab the groaning Sebring seven times. Meanwhile Frykowski, whose hands have been bound with a towel, manages to free himself and engage in a struggle with Atkins who has been guarding him.

As Frykowski stumbles toward the front door his escape is interrupted by Watson who pistol-whips him over the head multiple times, breaking the gun's right grip in the process. In the massive bloodshed occurring during this scene, a broken gun grip might seem to be a minor piece of the puzzle. But down the road, matching those broken pieces to a recovered murder weapon will become a significant piece of the investigation.

After pistol whipping Frykowski, Watson stabs him repeatedly. Amazingly at this point, Frykowski is still alive but Watson's attention is diverted to assist Krenwinkel in squelching an escape attempt by Abigail Folger, who has managed to flee out a bedroom door onto the front yard. After Krenwinkel catches her and tackles her to the ground, Watson proceeds to finish off the job. Folger is stabbed a total of 28 times.

Although having been shot and stabbed multiple times, Frykowski is still staggering across the front lawn toward the gate. The big guy goes down hard. Catching up with him, Watson pistol-whips Frykowski to the ground before finishing him off with a final flurry of stabbings. The autopsy report will indicate that Voytek Frykowski, in addition to 51 stab wounds, has also been struck in the head with a blunt object 13 times and shot twice.

The last to die is Sharon Tate who offers herself as a hostage until her baby is born. Unfortunately, the hostage option is not one that will be on the table this evening. Tate dies while pleading with Tex Watson and Susan Atkins for the life of her unborn child; she has been stabbed 16 times. Later, in jail, Atkins will boast about tasting Tate's blood, describing it as warm and sticky, and say that she thought about cutting out the baby but didn't have time.

> *There once was a girl Sexy Sadie*
> *Who after she stabbed Sharon Tate she*
> *Hoped that you knew*
> *The rumors weren't true*
> *She never did cut out the baby*

As they begin to depart Cielo Drive to head home, Susan Atkins, aka "Sexy Sadie", remembers Charles Manson's instructions to, "leave a sign... something witchy."[3] She subsequently goes back inside and grabs a strip of cloth that had been used to bind the victims during the murders. Atkins then dips the cloth in Sharon Tate's blood, comes back outside, and writes "Pig" on the front door. After that they head back to Spahn Ranch. There would be more work to do tomorrow.

One of the more interesting books we read in researching this piece was a 1977 book by Susan Atkins (Sexy Sadie) called *Child of Satan, Child of God*. By the time she wrote the book, Atkins had become a born-again Christian. That development, in a way, completed a "circle of life" scenario for her. As a child, she had won her church's award for achieving the greatest number of Gold Stars on Sunday School worksheet assignments.

At any rate, her book is unique in that she approaches the topic through a perspective of contrition, analyzing her actions with honesty. But the other piece she brings to the party is that obviously she was there, and she knows things that no one else knows.

Playing upon that last statement here is a nuance from the night of the Tate murders that in our years of research we never came across anywhere else. Upon their return to Spahn Ranch Charlie summons Tex inside the bunkhouse for a private conference. Curious, Atkins sidles closer to the door and hears the following conversation.

CHARLIE: Did you go to the next house?
TEX: No.
CHARLIE: *(obviously angry)* I told you to go to every house on that
             street. Now we'll have to go back.
TEX: It was crazy… everything went wild… [4]

So this does add an even scarier scenario as to how that night might have played out. Not that there's a huge body of comparisons, but by mass murder standards, the killing crew at the Tate house does not operate like a well-oiled machine. By the end you've got multiple victims, some of whom have escaped temporarily, lying all over the compound.

It's a rather repulsive thought to know that if these five victims had fallen quickly like dominoes, the plan was for the murder spree to have continued right around the block in some harrowing Halloween happening taking the form of the most turbulently twisted trick-or-treat turmoil ever.

THE AFTERMATH ⁓ Upon the departure of the Manson murder crew, the eerie silence originally noted by Sexy Sadie/Susan Atkins returns. As Sexy Sadie had noticed upon their entrance to the compound, "It was so quiet you could almost hear the ice cubes rattling in the cocktail glasses down in the canyon."

Suppose it were to become possible to time travel back to an infamous location, at the precise moment in time when that location achieved its infamy. This would be the scene at 10050 Cielo Drive shortly after midnight on the morning of August 9, 1969. Inside the house are two dead bodies, three if you'd like to include the unborn eight-and-a-half-month-old fetus being carried inside the womb of Sharon Tate.

Outside the residence are three more dead bodies; two sprawled out on the front lawn and one slumped over a steering wheel in the driveway. If one could have gone back in time and peered upon the compound from the street with unknowing innocence, it might have appeared as a serene scene surrounded by summer silence.

In that summer silence, a visual juxtaposition to winter could be vividly noted. There is a split rail fence, enclosing a patio on the left-hand side of the house. The previous residents, Terry Melcher and Candice Bergen, had run Christmas lights along that fence which, having never been taken down, now seem to add a somewhat subversively surrealistic sense of Christmas color to the silent scene.

Because of the angle of the California topography, the Cielo Christmas lights can be seen all the way from Sunset Strip. On this particularly portentous night, while life on the Strip never stops, here on Cielo Drive it has. It may have been a silent night, but it certainly was not a holy one.

(to the tune of "Silent Night")

Silent Night,
Deadly Night,
Sharon lies dead
Bleeding bright red
What a sad site to see Mother and child
Losing their lives to the vicious and wild
Despite bloodletting release
This daft plan won't end in peace

CHAPTER 9:
THE LABIANCA MURDERS
(AUGUST 9-11, 1969)

BACK TO THE RANCH ~ On their way home, the killer crew stops to ditch their bloody clothes and weapons. While Linda Kasabian is driving, the other three Family members change out of their bloody clothes and into clean sets that they had brought. Upon completion of the change, Kasabian pulls over and throws the clothes into a ravine. So as not to leave all the evidence in one place the weapons are discarded in different locations.

Keep this piece in mind because months later the facts surrounding the discovery of this evidence will serve to achieve two significant purposes. #1) It will help solve the crimes. #2) It will help characterize the quality, or lack thereof, of the police work in this case.

After the years we spent researching this book, perhaps the only thing more unbelievable than Charles Manson's theory of Helter Skelter is the shocking ineptitude with which the police agencies in Los Angeles handle the case. The screw-ups of the police agencies in L.A. as they follow this case in a manner which is ironically reflective of the Hollywood Keystone Cops. We will return to this topic later and elaborate on the details.

Meanwhile, upon hearing the news of how the Tate murders went down, Manson is disappointed that it does not create the panic he had hoped for. He also feels the mission was too sloppy, what with some bodies inside, some bodies outside and another slumped over in a car in the driveway. Subsequently, he decides his crew needs an onsite director and Manson will be along for the ride the following night.

HITTING L.A. FOR ROUND #2 ~ On the evening of August 9th, the Manson murder crew sets out for a second night of murder and mayhem. The cast of characters, includes the four from the previous night, as well as Charlie, Steve "Clem" Grogan and Leslie Van Houten, a 19-year old former homecoming queen who has recently joined the Family.

The second evening's targets are chosen in a basically random process. With Linda Kasabian at the wheel, their first stop is in a middle-class neighborhood. After leaving for a reconnaissance mission Charlie returns indicating that this wouldn't be a good choice because the houses are too close together.

They drive around the block scoping out possibilities and the next stop turns out to be one of a few rare examples of Charles Manson showing human compassion. They stop at a house and watch as Charlie goes up and peers in the window. After returning from this recon mission Charlie again indicates that this would not be their best choice. Through the window Charlie has seen pictures of children which dissuades him from turning this into the night's house of murder. He does go on to warn, however, that at some point in the future they may have to start killing children.

During the evening drive, Charlie also initiates a few more freelance killings, neither of which pan out for him. At one point he has Kasabian pull into a church parking lot and park the car as Charlie announces, "I'm going to kill the priest and hang him upside down on the cross."[1] A moment later Charlie returns with the (un)fortunate news that the church is locked.

Later that night the group notices an expensive sleek sports car driving ahead of them. "At the next red light, pull up beside it," Charlie says, "I'm going to kill the driver."[2] When Kasabian stops at the next traffic light, Charlie jumps out of their car and approaches the other vehicle when fatefully, the light turns green and the sports car zips off into the night. Somewhere in L.A. is a sports car driver who has no idea how close he was to death.

THE LABIANCAS ~ At this point Charlie determines that it's time to get down to business. They make their way to one of the more ritzy neighborhoods in L.A. and successfully target their next house. The victims of the night would be a couple in their mid-40's, millionaires Leno and Rosemary LaBianca. Having just returned from a stay in their lake house, their car and boat are still parked in the driveway. Too bad they hadn't stayed another night.

Manson and Watson initially break into the house, taking the couple by surprise. After putting pillowcases over their heads, they bind them with lamp cords before returning to the car. At this point Manson divides his team in half sending Watson, Krenwinkel and Van Houten in to take care of the LaBiancas. This three-person hit squad is directed to hitchhike home after the deed is done as the others are hitting the road in search of more Manson murder and mayhem.

After the three enter the LaBianca house, Watson tells Krenwinkel and Van Houten to go into the kitchen and get knives. The girls then take Mrs. LaBianca into the bedroom and, as LaBianca cries out for her husband, the girls take turns stabbing her in the back and buttocks. The coroner's report will indicate a total of 41 stab wounds on the body of Rosemary LaBianca.

Meanwhile in the living room, Tex Watson is using a bayonet to kill Leno LaBianca. With his larger, more efficient weapon, Tex is able to get the job done by stabbing his victim just 12 times. Then Krenwinkel comes in and stabs Mr. LaBianca 14 more times, bringing his grand total to 26, still 15 shy of his wife's final tally.

Krenwinkel leaves a two-tined fork jutting out of his stomach before plunging a carving knife into LaBianca's throat. Demonstrating his flair for always knowing how to put that perfect cherry on the top of a murder, Tex Watson then carves the word "WAR" into the exposed flesh of LaBianca's abdomen.

> *After just getting home with their boat*
> *Comes a problem that we must emote*
> *As murders are thundering*
> *Leno's a-wondering*
> *Is that a knife or a frog in my throat?*

After killing their victims, the trio reward themselves suitably. Taking advantage of the cushy facilities at the LaBianca home, the three of them cook a meal and have dinner. Fully satiated, Watson,

Krenwinkel and Van Houten have one task to complete before they shower; you know how messy those mass murders can be.

Krenwinkel then steps up to assume the role of group secretary. She dips a napkin in blood and on the wall writes "Rise" and "Death to Pigs". On the refrigerator she scrawls "Helter Skelter". Then they hitchhike back to Spahn Ranch. Charlie will be proud.

THE "B" TEAM ~ Remember Manson had been present at the beginning of the LaBianca killings; he had broken into the house to help subdue the couple before leaving. So where does Charlie go? Here's the second half of that night's story.

It is Manson's goal to have murders committed at multiple sites that night. To that end, after leaving Watson, Atkins and Krenwinkel at the LaBianca home, Charlie takes Steve "Clem" Grogan, Leslie Van Houten and Linda Kasabian, and the B-Team hits the road.

Manson has strategically kept Kasabian in the car for two reasons. #1) She is the only person left in the Manson Family that actually has a valid driver's license, and #2) He knows that Kasabian is an acquaintance of an actor who lives nearby. Charlie's hoping to use this to get easy access to another high profile Helter Skelter victim.

Following Manson's orders to go to the actor's apartment, Kasabian drives there but intentionally knocks on the wrong door, waking up a stranger and subsequently aborting yet another murder. The fact that Linda Kasabian is Manson's only legal driver is an anomaly that is unknowingly compromising Charlie's objectives. As we saw just above, Kasabian cleverly curtailed the murder attempt of the previous evening. Kasabian is clearly beginning to show a separation of values with Manson. That she is diverging from his influence can be confirmed below.

The only major move Manson makes in the days after the LaBianca murders is to facilitate a foray into a black section of L.A. where his plan is to ditch Rosemary LaBianca's wallet and credit cards in a spot where they are likely to be discovered by a black person. Manson hopes whoever discovers the wallet will subsequently use the credit cards, thereby establishing a link between the LaBianca murders and the black community. The goal is to help spark the rage in the white community that is needed to bring on Helter Skelter.

On this night, after driving Manson into a black section of the city, Charlie directs Kasabian to pull into a gas station. He then orders her to go into the women's bathroom and leave the wallet and credit cards where they will be easily found. Appearing to be following Manson's orders, Kasabian does go into the women's bathroom but rather than leaving the wallet out in the open, she hides it inside the tank of the toilet.

The wallet will eventually be found, but not until December. Two days later Linda Kasabian will escape the Manson Family and return home. This subplot will be covered later in the book.

CHAPTER 10:
THE INVESTIGATION BEGINS
(AUGUST 9-16, 1969)

In researching this story of the Tate-LaBianca murders committed by the Manson Family in 1969, a tangential storyline that significantly surprised us was the prevailing preponderance of police ineptitude which characterized the investigation. Let's start with an analysis of the relationship between the Los Angeles Police Department and the Los Angeles Sheriff's Office. This relationship is an important one because the rivalry between these two branches of law enforcement considerably contributes to the dysfunctional process that characterized the investigation.

The difference between these two law enforcement organizations is fairly straight forward. The Los Angeles Police Department (LAPD) is responsible for what happens within the city limits. The Los Angeles Sheriff's Office (LASO) is responsible for what happens within the county of Los Angeles, but outside the city limits.

So while the outline of responsibility is straightforward, it's understandable that certain crimes are going to overlap the geographic boundaries of these two agencies. For the most part that wouldn't necessarily be a problem. But the Tate-LaBianca murders were different.

The cases were so high profile that a level of jealousy developed creating a situation where evidence was not as readily shared as it should have been. Each agency was hopeful that it would be the one whose detective work would serve to crack the cases and subsequently enable it to be the agency that would bask in the glow of the inevitable accolades which would certainly be forthcoming.

In addition to the departmental rivalry between the LAPD and the LASO there was also an interdepartmental rivalry between the investigative teams assigned to the Tate murders and the LaBianca murders. A key fact to keep in mind at this point, as well as the cornerstone to the police ineptitude storyline, is that despite the obvious similarities the LAPD chooses to conduct its investigations upon the premise that the two multiple murders are unrelated.

Add to this the fact that early on in the investigations both the Tate and LaBianca teams allowed themselves to become locked into working theories as to what was the basic criminal motivation behind their particular investigation. And both teams would turn out to be wretchedly wrong.

The Tate team was focused on the drug angle. Various drugs were found in various locations in the house and vehicles. This made it easy for the police to focus on the high-profile Hollywood lifestyles of the rich and famous and adopt a theory of "live freaky, die freaky". The Tate team was certain that drugs were somehow related to the crime.

The LaBianca team was fixated on the fact that Leno was a gambler who liked to play the horses. They subsequently were lured into a Mafia/gambling theme. And despite the obvious similarities, each team was convinced that its murders were not connected to the other team's, except perhaps for some kind of copycat factor.

And here's the real kicker... remember the Gary Hinman murder? That one was being investigated by LASO. After the Tate-LaBianca murders, LASO called LAPD and said that they thought they had something LAPD could use. Gary Hinman had been stabbed to death and "political piggy" had been written in blood on the wall. The Tate murders were stabbings and "pig" was written in blood on the door and the LaBianca murders had been stabbings with "death to pigs" written in blood on the wall.

UNBELIEVABLY, the LAPD came to the decision that the three murder scenes were all unrelated. The Tate team continued to focus on the drug theory leading one to believe that perhaps they themselves were on drugs. The LaBianca team continued to focus on the gambling theme which was a gamble that would not pay off.

About this situation former L.A. County Deputy District Attorney Stephen Kay said, "The LAPD should have made that connection. The thing would have been solved in a few days."[1] The LAPD was basically gifted with the answer to the crime on the second day of the investigation and chose to do nothing with the gift.

On Monday, August 11, quotes from various LAPD officers confirm the fact that the department is progressing on the theory that there is no connection between the Tate and LaBianca murders. Sergeant Bryce Houchin says, "There is a similarity but whether it's the same suspect or a copycat we just don't know." Inspector K.J. McCauley adds, "I don't see any connection between this [Tate] murder and the others [LaBianca]. They're too widely removed." LAPD spokesman Lieutenant Dan Cooke summed up the department's stance on the crimes by saying, "The homicides are not connected."[2]

WILLIAM GARRETSON ~ The primary suspect, in fact the only suspect, in the Tate murders during the hours after the discovery of the crime is one William Garretson, who is the 19-year-old caretaker living in the guest house on the property where the murders have occurred. Obviously, in retrospect, we know he doesn't have anything to do with it, but with five gruesomely murdered victims, four of them lying dead within a hundred feet of him, Garretson is a person of interest.

Garretson is arrested and taken downtown for questioning. The biggest reason the police suspect him is the question of how could he have been so close to something so noisy and chaotic and not have heard anything? His answer—that he had his stereo on. A thought occurring to us that might have led the police to not totally jump to the conclusion that he was the killer would be to say this. If he had just murdered five people, would he be casually sitting on his couch watching television waiting for the police to arrive?

In questioning by the police Garretson reveals that Steven Parent had stopped over the previous night as Parent had a clock radio he was hoping Garretson might be interested in buying. He says they had a few beers, smoked some pot, and he thinks it had been a little after midnight when Parent left. The time on the clock radio when it is recovered by the police reads 12:15 am which seems to corroborate Garretson's story. If Parent had set the clock for demonstration purposes and unplugged it upon his departure, the 12:15 time would jive with the estimated time of the murders.

While swearing that he was aware of nothing unusual happening the previous night, Garretson does admit to the police that he felt a little scared. When asked why he said that, at one point after Parent had left, he had tried to make a phone call but noticed the line was dead. Shortly thereafter he had briefly left the guesthouse and upon his return noticed that the outside door handle was turned down, as if someone had tried to get in.

However, in the minds of the police, the moment of truth is rapidly approaching. Garretson has agreed to take a lie detector test which will in all likelihood dictate their next move. Of course, Garretson passes the polygraph, subsequently reducing the LAPD's pool of viable suspects from one to zero.

BUSTED ~ As the Family is laying low in the days after the Tate-LaBianca murders, the police close in on Spahn Ranch to round up the entire Manson Family on August 16. Susan Atkins remembers waking up to the sound of metal clicking upon metal and recalling, "I opened my eyes and looked into the barrel of a rifle aimed at my head. Holding it was a man who looked like a combination of astronaut and frogman."[3]

The ostentatious attire at which Atkins is staring is the uniform of a member of the L.A. SWAT team. The officer pointing the rifle at her head is one of 200 who had been assigned to conduct this raid of the Manson Family on the Spahn Ranch. "It's all over,"[4] Atkins thinks, but before you agree with her too quickly please patiently hear us out on a few related thoughts.

First off, the vast scope of the police assignment which has sent some 200 SWAT team members on this raid may have been a bit of overkill. The 200 officers arrest just two dozen people. That being said, if this police raid was to bring down the culprits behind the most notorious crime spree in L.A. history, the overkill would be easy to justify. But sweet ~~Manson~~ Jesus, the police are not here for the reason you're thinking.

Understandably, the initial fear of everybody, including Manson, is that they have been linked to the murders, but how's this for irony? The entire crew has been brought in for suspicion of car theft. Then, because of an incorrect date, the warrant is invalidated and the entire group is released. The LAPD actually has all the murderers in custody at one point and then just lets them go! It's been one week since the murders and at this point the police do not have a clue. Following is our limerick on Susan Atkins/Sexy Sadie's take on the raid.

> *Is that a frogman or an astronaut?*
> *For exactly what have I been caught?*
> *Scare the shit out of me*
> *Then just set me free*
> *This entire raid's all gone for naught*

KASABIAN ESCAPE ~ Unbeknownst to the police, however, there has been one very positive development in the week since the Tate-LaBianca murders went down. Linda Kasabian has managed to break free from the Manson Family. Ultimately, she will become the star witness for the prosecution. Perpetuating a theme which characterizes this storyline would be the fact that every positive development which happens for the police occurs outside the realm of their efforts.

The night after the LaBianca murders, Linda Kasabian makes the decision that she is going to try to escape from the Manson Family. This will be difficult because there are too many people around during the day and armed guards are posted at night. Throw in the fact that Kasabian also has a one-year old daughter named Tanya on the compound and, as per Manson's dictum, her child is being cared for by other women. It's clear that a successful escape, with her child, is not going to be easy.

On August 11, the day after the LaBianca murders, Manson assigns Kasabian to an area in the center of the compound precluding an attempted escape that day, and she is afraid to leave at night because of the guards. Early the next morning, which is August 12, Manson seeks her out and assigns her the task of driving to Sybil Brand Prison and delivering a message to Family members Mary Brunner and Sandra Good. The message just tells them to say nothing and everything's alright, which is typical of the messages Manson frequently sends to members of the Family who are incarcerated.

Upon arrival at the women's prison, Kasabian is informed that Brunner and Good are in court that day. After returning to the ranch to inform Manson that her mission has been unsuccessful, she is told to make another attempt the next day. Opportunity knocks.

That evening she packs supplies for Tanya and herself and hides the bag until the next morning. Early on August 13, Kasabian rises hoping to successfully execute her exit strategy, but things do not quite fall into place. Of all things, Manson himself is actually sleeping in the room where she had stowed the bag and she also finds out that the children have been moved to a new location in the center of the compound which makes it impossible for her to get Tanya out.

Faced with a difficult decision, Kasabian is so desperate to escape the maniacal mayhem of Manson's murderous mentality she decides to flee, leaving Tanya behind. Feeling she may never again be presented with a carte blanche opportunity to drive away from the ranch, with no one else in the car, she decides to seize the opportunity.

Kasabian drives from California to Albuquerque, New Mexico where her husband Bob Kasabian lives. Linda arrives to find Bob living in a commune with another woman. Not exactly the episode of the 1969 hit TV series *Love American Style* she had been hoping for. Feeling she has no choice, Linda tells her husband the entire story of the Tate-LaBianca murders and that Tanya is still back at the cult compound. Bob's response is that the two of them should drive to Spahn Ranch together and retrieve Tanya.

Aspersions are cast upon that plan, however, when Linda informs Bob that if they were to attempt that, she feels sure Manson will kill them all. Pondering a Plan B, Bob says that he needs a few days to weigh their options. But at that point Linda decides to be proactive and take things into her own hands.

She drives to Taos, New Mexico to meet with a man named Joe Sage. Sage is a quirky character who perennially runs for President of the United States on an anti-pollution platform. He also presides over his Macrobiotic Church which espouses a Taoist philosophy featuring the Eastern principles of yin and yang. Nice work if you can get it.

Sage is also known as a man who is willing to come to the aid of less fortunate people who have encountered problems and are in need of assistance. It is Kasabian's hope that her storyline of, "I've just been a reluctant participant in two mass murders and the cult for which I committed the crimes is holding my baby hostage on a movie ranch in California," will be a story that would clearly convey the need for assistance. If nothing else, she feels sure it will be a storyline that Joe Sage has never heard before.

That assumption on the part of Kasabian proves correct. She feels she has no choice but share all the details of the murders, getting all her cards out there on the table, in order for Sage to best consider their options. Perhaps not surprisingly, Sage does not believe the twisted tale he has been told, but he does agree to call Spahn Ranch on her behalf.

After dialing up the ranch, Sage first speaks to a girl, probably Squeaky. He is then passed on to Manson and the two men have a conversation. Can you imagine the lump in Manson's throat when Sage comes out and recites verbatim Kasabian's firsthand account of the two murderous nights in which she was involved? Manson resorts to basically the only defense option available for him by saying that Kasabian is delusional and disavows the story completely.

At this point it might seem that the phone call will prove to be a total waste of time but that turns out not to be the case. Manson returns the phone to Squeaky who in turn asks to speak to Linda. Squeaky shares with her the details of the August 16 raid and lets her know that Tanya was kept by the authorities. So while Squeaky can't confirm Tanya's whereabouts, she can convey the concept that the child is safe.

The phone call ends with Patricia Krenwinkel getting on the line and blasting Kasabian's betrayal. Krenwinkel screams, "You just couldn't wait to open your big mouth, could you?"[6] Two points to make at this time. First, imagine how rattled the cages must have been in the Manson camp to know the story of the murders was so far out there. And second, given that the story is so far out there, how can it still be two months before the police will figure it out?

Returning to the Tanya Kasabian storyline, Linda immediately calls the authorities in Los Angeles asking for assistance in locating her daughter. After being provided with the name of the social worker handling Tanya's case, another intriguing detail arises, and this one's a little eerie.

When Linda Kasabian makes contact with the social worker, she is informed that someone has just visited the agency posing as Tanya's mother and attempting to claim the child. Because the woman did not possess adequate proof of parenthood, the child was not released. The logical theory on this would be that Manson had sent one of his girls to the agency in an attempt to get Tanya back so the child could be used as leverage to prevent Kasabian from telling her story.

While Joe Sage seemingly never believes Kasabian's account of events, he does provide her with enough money for round trip airfare to Los Angeles and the name of an L.A. attorney, Gary Fleischman, who can help reunite her with her daughter. After a court appearance, that reunion is realized and mother and daughter fly back to Taos.

Upon returning to New Mexico, Kasabian is able to affirm that her husband Bob is still involved with the other woman. Subsequently in late October, pregnant and transporting a one-year-old baby, she hitchhikes from New Mexico to Miami, Florida where her father lives. When things don't work out there, in early November she hitchhikes to Concord, New Hampshire where her mother lives.

On December 2, 1969, a newsflash reveals that she has been implicated in the Tate-LaBianca murders. The writing is on the wall, although this time it's not in blood. Linda Kasabian turns herself in, waives extradition, and is flown back to Los Angeles.

NEWSPAPER CRAZINESS ~ The Sunday, August 17 edition of the *LA Times* features some coincidental craziness that is not comprehended by anyone in the city at the time. Check out the three stories that all appear on the front page. The headline story is about the Tate killings. Nine days after the murders had occurred the lead story is still, "ANATOMY OF A MASS MURDER IN HOLLYWOOD". Below that article is a smaller one with the headline, "LABIANCA COUPLE, VICTIMS OF SLAYER, GIVEN FINAL RITES". Keep in mind, at this point, the police, almost unbelievably, have established no connection between the Tate and LaBianca murders.

But here's the really ironic kicker. On the left side of that same page is a story about the Manson Family, bearing the headline "POLICE RAID RANCH, ARREST 26 SUSPECTS IN AUTO THEFT RING."[1] This triumvirate of stories are the three main dots connecting all the key players in what Vincent Bugliosi, who will eventually become the prosecutor in the trial, refers to as, "probably the most publicized murder case in history, excepting only the assassination of President John F. Kennedy."[2]

Talk about fate working in strange ways. If someone could have only played connect the dots with the newspaper that morning. The three pieces in this legendary story are touching each other, literally. Those connections which, despite their greatest efforts the police will not make for months to come, are connected solely through a twist of fate in the *LA Times* that day.

Here's a final irony that places an appropriate cherry on the top of this story, while also serving to punctuate police ineptitude. Because the police have incorrectly dated the auto theft warrant, two days later the entire Family is released. Here the police have managed to arrest everyone involved in the most high-profile crime in the city's history and two days later they let them all go never realizing what they had. The release of the Manson Family does not even make the paper.

> *Gotta laugh at the LAPD*
> *They arrest the whole Family tree*
> *Police work abhorrent*
> *They misdate the warrant*
> *And let all the killers go free*

SHORTY SHEA ~ Of the nine murders unequivocally attributed to the Manson Family, Donald "Shorty" Shea has the distinction of being the last. Shorty is a 36-year-old ranch hand who has drifted on and off of the Spahn Ranch for the past decade and in his autopsy report he is identified as "foreman" of the ranch. One of the few remaining non-Manson personnel, Shorty has often given negative feedback to George Spahn about the antics of the Manson cult on his property.

In addition to Shorty's concerns about the Manson takeover of the Spahn Ranch, there are also some underlying differences between the two men. Shorty had married a black topless dancer and Manson has always been opposed to interracial marriages.

Manson hated the blacks, the cops and the establishment. Who he hated most would be a tough call but in Charlie's jargon, if you were blackie, the pigs, or the piggies you were on Charlie's shit list and Shorty's stock certainly did not go up in Manson's eyes when he married a black chick.

And while Shorty's negative intuitions about the Mansons prove to be spot on, put yourself in George's position. He's 80-years old, virtually blind, and needs some consistent help. Charles Manson has assigned as George's personal assistant 19-year old Lynette "Squeaky" Fromme who is directed to provide for his every need. So while the transient Shorty comes and goes, Squeaky just comes.

While the preliminary territory of tensions between Charlie and Shorty had been drawn up long ago, the fact that Manson suspects Shorty of being the snitch behind the August 16 raid proves to be the last straw. Plans are made to assure Shorty will soon be short on time.

In the aftermath of the August 16 bust, Shorty again visits George to voice his concerns about the Manson Family. His timing is right in every way but one. Given the fact that the entire Family, as well as all the ranch hands, have been recently arrested, it would seem appropriate for George to perhaps reconsider the arrangement he has offered Charles Manson.

That's the component where Shorty's timing is right. The part that turns out wrong is that, unbeknownst to Shorty, Squeaky is within earshot of the conversation. So keep in mind that in her duality of responsibilities, while serving as the eyes for the nearly-blind Spahn, she is also serving as the ears for the completely crazy Manson.

After hearing of Shorty's most recent attempt to sabotage his status with the Spahn Ranch, Manson confirms his decision to assure there will be a shortage in Shorty's remaining days. Whether it is true or not, Manson feels that Shorty is behind the August 16 raid, as well he may have been.

On August 26, Shorty is convinced to ride with Tex Watson, Bruce Davis and Steve "Clem" Grogan to a nearby car parts yard. The reason they called him Shorty and not Smarty becomes evident at this point. Knowing what has transpired recently, you might suspect Shorty would be reluctant to head out on a field trip with a trio of Manson members. After Clem clubs him over the head with a pipe wrench and Watson stabs him, it probably doesn't take long for Shorty to realize that this ride is not going to go down as one of his better decisions. Probably his worst since the decision to read *The Pop-Up Book of Phobias*; what could possibly go wrong?

After arriving at their desired destination, he is dragged out of the car, stabbed and brutally tortured to death. At this point, his body is dismembered with various participants in the murder establishing the range of the number of pieces into which the body has been cut to be somewhere between six and nine. But what the hell, who's counting?

They clubbed him and shouted a curse word
But help pleas from Shorty went unheard
He claimed he's no snitch
But son of a bitch
He wound up completely dismembered

TABLOID TITILLATIONS ⁓ As the dog days of August begin to wind down to a close, the police remain unable to make any arrests or even develop any promising leads. Given this scenario, the media is provided with free reign to espouse theatrical theory and convoluted conjecture. The wealthy high-profile victims of the Tate murders make for easy targets, ironically for the second time around. After being initially killed by Manson, they are subsequently murdered by the media.

We are going to begin our coverage of this component by sharing some responsible journalism. Before we stoop to the depths of sensationalistic publications such as *The Globe* and *National Enquirer*, here is the journalistic analysis of *The New York Times*, a publication which, at least from a relative perspective, could be considered one of the adults in the room.

The *Times* summarizes the situation by saying, "all the stories have a common thread – that somehow the victims have brought the murders upon themselves." Their premise is that if you live a life-in-the-fast-lane lifestyle permeated with sex and drugs, don't be surprised if something goes wrong. The *Times* concludes their coverage by writing, "the attitude is summed up in the epigram: 'Live freaky. Die freaky'."[3] In the following paragraphs, we'll break down the "freak factor" characterizing each of the celebrities involved.

SHARON TATE ⁓ Think of the material that the sensationalist tabloid publications have to work with here. Sharon Tate had been in her bedroom, sitting on the bed with former lover Jay Sebring, 8½ months pregnant, wearing just a bra and panties, while her husband Roman Polanski was in Europe. Not exactly middle America in the 1960's.

Sebring's sexual quirkiness had long been fodder for the Hollywood rumor mill, as was the case with Polanski. By virtue of the fact that Sebring and Polanski had been her last two lovers, Sharon Tate immediately fell victim to the guillotine of guilt by association. Not that it was our goal but, after having already been murdered by the Mansons, then the media, we think we may have just killed her for the third time.

ROMAN POLANSKI ⁓ And in terms of being a sitting duck for a good Hollywood hazing, the targets don't get much easier than Roman

Polanski. Let's play a round of the hypothetical game Past Day, Modern Day. In the "Past Day" round of the game, let's throw out the question, "For what is Roman Polanski most famous?" The answer would be his obsession with sex and his fascination with the macabre.

In the "Modern Day" round we'll ask, "Why has nobody in the United States seen Roman Polanski in the last 40 years?" The answer would be that after pleading guilty to statutory rape for drugging and raping a 13-year-old girl in 1978 he fled to France while awaiting sentencing.[4]

During the past four decades Polanski has continued a prolific film production career in France. International law is not a topic of much interest to us, nor one that we are likely to delve into again soon, but we do have one common thought on this situation.

Whatever the extradition laws are between the United States and France, please allow us to express the following opinion. If the existing laws don't allow for the extradition of someone convicted for drugging and raping a 13-year-old, someone really needs to rethink this.

ABIGAIL FOLGER AND VOYTEK FRYKOWSKI ~ Finalizing the explanation for why the Tate murder victims are all easy tabloid trashing targets, we'll complete the picture by dishing out the details on Abigail Folger and Voytek Frykowski. There does not seem to be a lot of depth to their relationship. Her greatest attribute is that she is rich, the heiress to the Folger coffee fortune. His greatest attribute is that he is built like a brick shithouse.

Before meeting Folger, Frykowski is a lifeguard who can't even speak English. If online dating services had been available in the '60's, Frykowski's overall profile certainly would not have been a babe magnet for hot millionaire chicks.

But after the initial attraction kicks in, the relationship is able to advance because they do both speak some French. That being said, we acknowledge that this is at least a bit more than a "me Tarzan, you Jane" relationship. Abigail embarks upon teaching English to Voytek, who subsequently makes it his admirable goal to become a screenwriter. Each of those goals is only modestly attained.

By the summer of '69 their relationship is clearly deteriorating with fighting and drug use both on the rise. That being said, they continue their Hollywood high, enjoying the prestige of co-hosting multiple parties throughout the summer at the home of Sharon Tate.

RECAPPING ~ So now, allow us to restate the primary point of the last several paragraphs. Since the police investigators have been totally inept at connecting the dots between any of the multiple leads out there waiting for them, the opportunity is laid wide open for sensationalist journalism to rear its ugly head. And the fact that the truly innocent victims were all enjoying lavish luxuriant high-profile Hollywood lifestyles makes the supersonic sales of the spurious stories soar astronomically.

Here are some samplings of the false news stories that permeate the papers. Sharon Tate is deemed "a dabbler in satanic arts" and also anointed as "the queen of the Hollywood orgy scene."[5] Can't help but wonder what type of oil would be used in that type of anointment; but don't worry, we're checking it out for you.

CHAPTER 12:
FINALLY FIGURING OUT WHO DID IT
(OCTOBER 10-DECEMBER 16, 1969)

RETURN TO THE VALLEY ~ Feeling the need to stay one step ahead of the law, Manson returns the Family to Barker Ranch, near Death Valley. The fact that so much time goes by before the Family gets busted for the murders is especially surprising given the sketchy background and general lack of discipline that characterized the crew. And as you've already seen, when Manson is first arrested it isn't even for the murders. There will be still more time before the authorities actually connect him to the Tate-LaBianca crimes. But we promise to deliver some big news by the end of this chapter.

At Barker Ranch the Family's primary recreational activity is stealing Volkswagen Beetles and converting them into dune buggies for resale. But of course car theft comes with a risk and Barker Ranch is raided on October 10 after investigators spot stolen cars on the property. Some of the evidence seized traces back to a previous arson arrest of Manson, who is not on site at the time of this raid.

The police however remain vigilante and arrest Manson when he returns to the ranch on October 12. The irony, of course, is that at this point, more than two months after the killings, no connection whatsoever has been made between Manson and the Tate-LaBianca murders. To the police, Manson is still just a fairly low-level criminal.

Just to help you keep your ranches straight, allow us to offer the following review. Spahn Ranch is the former Western movie set located near L.A. while Barker Ranch is located over two hundred miles away in Death Valley and is basically used by Manson as an L.A. getaway. The Tate-LaBianca murders were staged from Spahn Ranch. The New Year's Eve Helter Skelter prophesy was delivered at Barker Ranch. The August 16 raid where the Family was arrested and quickly released occurred at Spahn. The October 10 & 12 arrests occur at Barker.

As previously stated, the police do not initially connect the Tate and LaBianca murders despite their obvious similarities and proximity of time. They continue to focus on a drug theme for the Tate murders and a gambling theme for the LaBiancas, cripplingly convinced that the only connection in the crimes might be some kind of copycat killer conclusion. That narrow approach certainly contributes to the reality that the police are not able to complete a successful short-term investigation on their own. Ironically, in this case, it turns out to be one of the criminals that helps the police accomplish what they cannot on their own.

SEXY SADIE SAYS ~ It will actually be later in November before various pieces of evidence finally connect the dots between the two murder sprees. Susan Atkins has been scooped up in the October 10 raid at Barker Ranch. She will never see freedom again. Shortly after her incarceration, one of the Family members implicates her in the murder of Gary Hinman and she is charged with that crime and transferred from Death Valley to L.A. The police, however, are still clueless about her participation in both the Tate and LaBianca murders.

Sexy Sadie/Susan Atkins is subsequently incarcerated at the Sybil Brand Women's Prison. Ironically one of Charlie's favorite angels eventually becomes the driving factor in his demise. Whether it is her need for attention or her desire to elevate her status amongst her fellow inmates, Susan Atkins begins to brag about her criminal exploits with the Manson Family.

It is on the afternoon of November 6, when Susan Atkins first reaches the point where she becomes unable to contain herself regarding her involvement with the Tate-LaBianca murders. On that afternoon she sits down on the bed of her cellmate Virginia Graham and begins a leading conversation where Atkins will soon confide it all. In talking about the police Atkins says, "You know, there is a case right now; they are so far off the track they don't even know what's happening."

"What are you talking about?" Graham asks.

Atkins replies, "That one on Benedict Canyon."

"Benedict Canyon?" queries Graham, "You don't mean Sharon Tate?"

"Yeah," replies an increasingly excited Atkins, "You know who did it, don't you?" With her eyes aglow after hearing Graham respond in the negative, Atkins says, "Well, you're looking at her."[1]

After that the details come gushing out, leaving Graham in a sensationally stunned sense of shock. During her history of incarceration, this is certainly not the first time a fellow convict has confided a crime to her, but never before has there ever been anything like this. The enormity of this news is virtually overwhelming!

As Atkins confides the details of the crime, Graham's questions obviously drift toward the subject of motive and when offered the Helter Skelter explanation Atkins' confidante finds herself sitting in stunned silence. Just try and put yourself in Graham's place for a moment. You've just become privy to the details of one of the most famous unsolved murders in history.

Sitting on your bed beside you is the murderess who actually inflicted the stab wounds which killed Sharon Tate and her unborn baby. What do you do with that? In the aftermath of the confession, Graham is conflicted. Snitching is of course strictly forbidden within the code of jailhouse conduct. But isn't this something different?

The next day Virginia Graham confides Susan Atkins' confession to her closest jailhouse friend, Ronnie Howard. Howard is understandably skeptical of the Atkins' story and how's this for irony? Howard actually knows Tate murder victim Jay Sebring, having met him through a friend who worked for Sebring as a manicurist.

With two women now in the loop on the Atkins confession, Graham and Howard spend the next few days discussing and debating what their course of action should be. Totally torn on the topic they decide to sit tight, at least temporarily. They will always be able to tell the story but once told they can never untell it. They agree upon a course of action whereby they will first try to determine if Atkins is actually telling the truth, but given their situation there is no clear-cut strategy toward achieving that goal.

On November 12, less than one week after Atkins' confession, this jailhouse scenario takes an unexpected twist. On that day Virginia Graham is informed that she is being transferred to another facility.

From this point forward, the two women will obviously be following independent paths in determining what they will do with the information which has been provided by Susan Atkins.

Before her departure, Graham is made privy to the future plans of the Manson Family. The group has compiled a hit list of celebrities who are to be the next to die. That list includes Frank Sinatra, Steve McQueen, Tom Jones, Elizabeth Taylor and Richard Burton.

And not only have the Mansons compiled their list, they've also done some sadistic style selection. Here's what Sexy Sadie shares:

TOM JONES ~ The plan was to have Tom go out with a smile on his face. Sadie would seduce him into making love with her. Then, just when Jones was achieving orgasm, Sadie would slit his throat. All this, we're sure, with "It's Not Unusual" playing in the background.

> *Sadie's plan does hope to have him*
> *Right on the verge of a spasm*
> *But just as Tom's coming*
> *Through his neck she's running*
> *A knife cutting short his orgasm*

FRANK SINATRA ~ This one shows a little more creativity. Knowing that Sinatra was a lady's man, the plan was to bring a bevy of bodacious Manson babes to his house one night and extend the offer of group sex. Picture the scene. With "Strangers in the Night" playing in the background Sadie and her gal pals would do their sexy slink up to the front door and surely Sinatra would invite them right in.

That, of course, would prove a costly mistake on Frank's part, "Somethin' Stupid" you might say. Safely inside, the girls would proceed to hang him upside down and skin him alive while they played one of his records in the background. "That's Life."

At that point it would be time for some arts and crafts. Just to assure that anyone who really wanted a piece of Frank would be able to have one, they would use his skin to fashion cute little change purses which they would market through the hippie stores around the country, all the way to "New York, New York."

Frank thought all the girls would be fun
He never thought he'd be hung
They peeled off his skin though
Much to his chagrin so
Those wanting a Frank purse could have one

ELIZABETH TAYLOR & RICHARD BURTON ~ Okay we admit it, we've saved the best for last. Having learned from the mistakes of the Tate murders, this operation would go much more smoothly; nobody would be escaping out onto the lawn during this one. To get the festivities started Dick and Liz would be tied up with a rope around their necks and their feet.

In killing Liz, Sadie would begin by leaving her mark. This would be accomplished by heating a knife until it was literally red hot and then putting the knife to the side of Taylor's cheek. Then she would gouge Liz's eyeballs out, the way Charlie had taught her. Finally, just so the message is clear, she would carve the words "Helter Skelter" into Taylor's forehead.

If there's any silver lining to be found here, at least eyeball-less Liz won't have to see what's going to happen next. Sadie would castrate Burton and look for that grandiose gesture to make just the right statement with the props she has assembled. She would take Elizabeth Taylor's eyes and Richard Burton's penis and put them in a jar which, get this, she would mail to Eddie Fisher. Won't Eddie be surprised?!

To Liz and Dick's theme, let's drink high balls
The murderous Mansons climbed high walls
Then Sadie'd burn Liz
And call it show biz
While planning to carve out her eyeballs

While the chicks loved his oral fixation
Dick Burton did fear his castration
Why Sadie you're shtick's sick
You just hacked off Dick's dick
There will be no more masturbation

With Graham gone from Sybil Brand Prison, Ronnie Howard becomes Atkins' go-to companion and she proceeds to share all the gruesome details of the murders which she had shared with Graham. It is at this point that Howard finally comes to a decision regarding her course of action.

"I never informed on anyone in the past," she later explains, "but this one thing I couldn't go along with. I kept thinking that if I didn't say anything these people would probably be set free. They were going to pick other houses, just at random. It could have been my house next time, or yours, or anyone's."[2]

The story gets rather quirky at this point. You would think that if somebody in jail wanted to report a crime to the authorities that it would be a pretty easy thing to do. Howard, however, finds out that is not the case. She tells a female deputy at the jail that she knows who committed the Tate-LaBianca murders and asks for permission to call LAPD. The deputy tells Howard that she will pass on that request to her superior.

After hearing nothing for three days, Howard asks the deputy about the status of her request. She is told that the superior doesn't believe there is anything to the story and suggests that it just be forgotten. Howard asks the deputy if she can make the call to LAPD for her but is told that would be against the rules at Sybil Brand Prison.

BACK TO GRAHAM – Let's return to the Virginia Graham thread of the story. Two days after her transfer to Corona Prison, on November 14, she comes to the conclusion that, although she is still skeptical of Susan Atkins' story, she wants to tell somebody just in case. Graham ironically encounters her own battle with behind-bars bureaucracy. The person at Corona who she has come to trust the most is a psychologist named Vera Dreiser. Protocol at Corona dictates that in order for an inmate to speak to a staff member a blue request form must be completed.

Graham completes the form adding the comment that it is very important for Dr. Dreiser to see her. That form is returned with the notation that in order to speak to Dr. Dreiser another form has to be sent to Dr. Owens who is the administrator of that unit. That second form comes back confirming the meeting with Dreiser... at a date specified in December. By then it will be too late.

NOW BACK TO HOWARD ~ On November 17, Ronnie Howard and some other inmates are being transported by bus from Sybil Brand to court appearances in Santa Monica. During this process the women are initially dropped off at the men's jail on Bouchet Street. Before the second leg of the journey they usually have a little time when each woman is allowed to use a payphone.

Seizing the opportunity, Howard gets in the phone line. When time begins to run out she bribes the two women in front of her in order to advance to the head of the line and get a call out. She calls the Beverly Hills Police Department and tells the responding officer that she knows who committed the Tate-LaBianca murders.

The officer tells Howard that case is being handled by the Los Angeles Police Department and her call should be directed to them. She subsequently calls LAPD, repeats her claim that she knows who committed the murders, and tells them that she will be in court that entire day. As she sits through her judicial session, she is visually assessing everyone in the courtroom, assuming that one of them is the officer that will debrief her before her departure. Unfortunately, court ends that day, no one speaks to her, and a frustrated Howard is taken on the bus back to jail.

But that evening Howard's frustrations are abated when two homicide officers from LAPD do arrive at Sybil Brand to question her. This becomes the breakthrough moment in the investigation as the officers depart for headquarters to share with their colleagues that they have cracked the case. Of course, there's an underlying irony hanging over the detective work that has been done in the case to this point.

At the upcoming press conference an LAPD spokesperson will seek to credit the department by citing the statistic that almost 10,000 man-hours have been devoted to the investigation. But the reality of the situation is that 101 days after the murder, the specific information leading to the case being cracked has nothing whatsoever to do with any of the police work.

POLICE INEPTITUDE ~ The ability to pin the crime on Manson is graciously given to the police, gloriously gift-wrapped, by one of his gregariously garrulous girls. Nearly three months after the Tate-LaBianca murders the cops finally figure it out, by no means due to their own adept police work, but only because one of the Manson girls has spilled her guts in prison.

As the police pat themselves on the back for their job well done, you know and we know that it's all basically self-serving bullshit. At the press conference lauding the fact that they cracked the case, while acknowledging all the man hours LAPD has poured into the investigation, there's a dime and some time they conveniently leave out of their news briefing. They don't even mention the specific event which led to the case being solved, namely that ten cent phone call and the two minutes it took for Virginia Graham to fill them in with the details about what really happened.

Problematic police work so preposterously permeates this investigation that to share it all would actually bog down the story, so right now we are going to illustrate this overall concept by detailing the LAPD's two most embarrassing days in the process. As fate would have it, these two days come back to back, on December 15 and 16, 1969.

EXAMPLE #1 ~ While driving home on Beverly Glen Road after the Tate murders, Tex Watson, Patricia Krenwinkel and Susan Atkins had changed out of their bloody clothes into new sets of clothing which had been brought along for just that purpose. In her confession Susan Atkins had shared the information that, "After changing clothes in the car, we drove along a steep embankment with a mountain on one side, ravine on the other. We stopped and Linda got out of the car and threw all the clothes, all drippy with blood, over the side."[3]

Using this information, on December 15 a news crew from L.A.'s KACB TV station decides to conduct an experiment. The four-man crew decides to create a reenactment in an attempt to determine where the discarded clothing may have ended up. Starting at the former Tate residence, they drive down Beverly Glen Road in the direction of the Spahn Ranch. As we visualize this experiment in our heads we can't help but chuckle a bit.

Picture the scene... you have four grown men in a car boasting the KACB-TV logo. One of them is driving and the other three, sitting beside each other, are about to change clothes with the vehicle in motion. On your mark, get set, start changing.

The goal of this slapstick charade is to determine approximately how far a vehicle could travel during the time it would take three people to simultaneously change from one set of clothes to another, with no particular sense of urgency at this point. In case we've enticed you into wanting to try this experiment on your own and you're wondering what would be a good time, here's your answer. It takes the news crew about six minutes.

Mission accomplished, they look for the first shoulder wide enough to allow them to pull the car completely off the road. Voila! Ravine on the left, mountain on the right, so they get out to take a look. Sure enough in looking down the ravine they see a dark pile of something about fifty feet below.

They begin to feel that "Oh, my God" pit in the bottom of their stomachs, thinking they may have stumbled onto something. Their exhilaration, however, is tempered by the notion that surely the LAPD would have searched likely locations for evidence. But of course, as opposed to you, they are not aware of how badly the LAPD has been underperforming in this investigation.

The slope is steep and these dudes are not mountain climbers. The newscaster, the cameraman, the sound man and the driver slowly descend the treacherous traverse eventually reaching a ten-foot-square area where there is indeed clothing strewn about. In gathering the items they find they have three sets of clothes and... drum roll... they're blood stained.

Obviously the LAPD is a little red-faced at this turn of events. Critical evidence, to which they have essentially been drawn a road map, has been located by a news crew rather than the police. We're predicting that on the sports report that night the score for this one would have been reported as follows. KACB 1 – LAPD 0.

EXAMPLE #2 – The key moment in this storyline occurs on December 16, 1969, but the plot actually begins a few months earlier on September

1. On that morning, 10-year-old Steven Weiss is out playing in his backyard. The Weiss backyard is an unusual one in that most of it consists of a steep slope that ascends to Beverly Glen Road up above.

While randomly climbing his steep backyard hill that morning, young Steven's eye is caught by a bright reflection emanating from something lying under a bush. Upon closer inspection, Steven realizes it is a gun. Returning home, Steven shows the gun to his father, Bernard Weiss who immediately calls the police. As he hands it over to the arriving officer, Bernard Weiss notices that the right gun grip is missing from the weapon.

We mentioned earlier, in Chapter 8, that Tex Watson had broken the gun grip when pistol whipping Voytek Frykowski during the Tate murders. LAPD had decided to not release to the press the information about the broken grip, strategizing that withheld information might be used to corroborate a story somewhere down the line. It's ironically appropriate that it takes a case of what you might call double ineptitude, and an assist from a private citizen, for the police to finally connect the dots on this one.

Someone in the LAPD leaked the information about the broken grip to the press. When Bernard Weiss sees this story, with the leaked information, his heart starts to race and on December 16, he makes what would have had to be an apprehensive phone call to the police. While his exact words are not on record anywhere, he would have had to essentially say, "You know that murder weapon you're looking for in the Manson case? I think I turned it over to you last September 1."

So, to summarize, the police have been looking for three months to find the murder weapon in the most high-profile crime in the history of the City of Los Angeles. It is only after a departmental leak, coupled by a phone call from a private citizen, do the police come to realize that the weapon in question had actually been in their possession for the past 2½ months.

CHAPTER 13:
THE TRIAL BEGINS
(FEBRUARY 26-JUNE 15, 1970)

Leading up to the trial, on February 26, 1970, a deal is signed offering complete immunity to Linda Kasabian in exchange for her testimony. The deal was offered for very logical reasons. Along with the most crazy-ass motive any jury will have ever heard, there is a lot of circumstantial evidence involved with this case. In order for the prosecution to be confident they are truly in command of the situation, they feel like they need to flip one of the Manson girls. That girl will be Linda Kasabian. The reason why is that... of the most involved, she is the least involved. The preceding is a statement that needs some explanation which we will now provide.

MOST INVOLVED WITH BOTH MURDERS ~ Linda Kasabian has been with the Family for a long time, having started out as one of Manson's most devoted followers or she would not have been assigned to the murder missions. She is present at both the Tate and LaBianca murder sites. Subsequently, she has firsthand knowledge and can provide eye witness testimony regarding both events.

LEAST INVOLVED AT TATE MURDERS ~ Recalling the details that we previously shared with you, as the Manson team approaches the Tate house, they notice a car coming down the driveway, headed toward them. Fearing they have been seen, Tex Watson stops the car and kills the driver.

Watson subsequently tells Kasabian to stay near the car and watch the gate while the others will go to the house and take care of business. This scenario results in the fact that she is not personally involved with any of the murders which take place at the Tate house.

LEAST INVOLVED AT LABIANCA MURDERS – At the LaBianca murder scene, Manson divides his crew in half and Kasabian is not in the half that goes to the LaBianca house. Manson leaves, strategically taking her with him, because he knows that Kasabian is an acquaintance of an actor who lives nearby.

Manson's goal is to locate somebody else famous to kill. Following Manson's directions to go to the actor's apartment, Kasabian drives there but intentionally knocks on the wrong door, awakening a stranger and subsequently aborting another murder.

THE TRIAL BEGINS – The trial begins on June 15, 1970, and not surprisingly the Manson Family turns it into an absolute freak show. Initially, despite emphatic warnings from the judge not to do so, Manson is allowed to act as his own attorney. The appeal of this scenario to Manson is obvious. As acting attorney, he has the right to interview witnesses, thus allowing him access to his co-defendants. How convenient is this?

Manson however uses his power of attorney recklessly, submitting a series of preposterous pre-trial motions, eventually resulting in the judge stripping him of the right to represent himself. To explain this concept, we'll share with you a couple of Manson's maniacal motions, the preposterousness of which we would like to properly portray.

One of Manson's requests is that he "be free to travel to any place I should deem fit in preparing my defense". Another is that the "Deputy District Attorneys in charge of the trial be incarcerated for a period of time under the same circumstances that I have been subject to."[1] Sorry Charlie, those things aren't going to happen, but something else will.

It all comes to a head during the second week of March when presiding Judge William Keene officially vacates Manson from his status as acting attorney. "It's not me that's on trial here," an infuriated Manson screams, "this court is on trial!" To the judge Manson adds, "Go wash your hands. They're dirty."[2]

LIEUTENANT PAUL WATKINS – There will be one more significant event related to the case which transpires before the end of March. One of the prosecution's key witnesses is Paul Watkins who was

Charles Manson's chief lieutenant for a period of time. The prosecution almost loses him when the Volkswagen camper in which he is sleeping bursts into flames.

At this point, we will float two possible theories for anyone who has become a member of the Manson Family. #1) Joining the Family inadvertently results in the possibility that your body may spontaneously combust causing the vehicle in which you are sleeping to burst into flames leading to your death. Or, #2) Joining the Family inadvertently leaves them with the desire to kill you if you depart ways. We're leaning toward choice #2.

Watkins is pulled out of the burning vehicle and taken to Los Angeles County General Hospital. The medical report indicates second degree burns over 25% of his face, arms and back. Just days before the event, county authorities had heard chatter indicating the Family intended to put out a hit on Watkins in order to prevent his testimony.

> *Far be it from me to inquire*
> *About things that could be called dire*
> *Is there anything worse than*
> *To wake up in your van*
> *And find out your ass is on fire?*

APRIL ~ On April 13, Charles Manson files an affidavit of prejudice against Judge William Keene asking that he be removed from the case. By California law, the defendant doesn't even have to give a reason and the judge can be automatically removed. Any defendant in the state has the right to employ this one-time opportunity at any point, and Charlie chooses to play that single card at this stage of the game. In this case, the replacement named is Judge Charles H. Older who will remain on the bench for the duration of the trial.

The other significant related event occurring during April is that Bobby Beausoleil will be found guilty for the murder of Gary Hinman. Previously, Beausoleil had tried unsuccessfully to pin the crime on Manson. The chief witness at the trial for the prosecution turns out to be Mary Brunner, the mother of Charles Manson's child.

There is one aspect of Brunner's testimony that worries Vincent Bugliosi, who has been appointed as prosecuting attorney in the Manson case. In her testimony, Brunner does everything within her power to absolve Manson. Bugliosi can't help but wonder… what lengths will Susan Atkins, Leslie Van Houten and Patricia Krenwinkel go through to try and protect their leader in the upcoming Tate-LaBianca trials?

MAY ~ As time progresses toward the June 15 date set for the beginning of the trial, there are some significant events which take place during the month of May. On May 25, while visiting the LAPD's evidence room, prosecuting attorney Vincent Bugliosi notices a large object leaning against the wall in the corner.

Upon approaching the item, closer inspection reveals a psychedelically painted wooden door. Inscribed upon the mural on the door is the phrase "1,2,3,4,5,6,7… All Good Children Go to Heaven" and also the words, "HELTER SKELTER IS COMING DOWN FAST". The Helter Skelter reference we're sure you all get. As explained in Bonus Chapter 1, the significance of the nursery rhyme line is that the Beatles use it in the song "You Never Give Me Your Money" which is one of the tracks Manson uses in his preaching.

A shocked Bugliosi inquires as to when this piece of evidence had been obtained. LAPD informs him that this door, which was retrieved from the Spahn Ranch on November 25, 1969, was never considered important enough to be booked into evidence. Had it been booked into evidence it would have appeared on the evidence lists systematically provided to all attorneys, including Bugliosi.

Vincent Bugliosi has spent the last several months trying to more firmly establish the connection between the Manson Family and the "Helter Skelter" motive. The fact that LAPD has had this door for so long without ever booking it into evidence adds to Bugliosi's frustration with the manner in which this case has been handled by the police.

If you're captivated by the freaky nuances of the notoriety of the Manson legend here's the best the month of May has to offer. While achieving national headlines, the entire country is so caught up in the cacophony that the press descends upon the accessible members of the

Manson Family (i.e. those not in jail) to the point where the girls and the reporters come to know each other on a first name basis.

Picture this hypothetical scenario; the Manson Family's Squeaky Fromme and ABC's Sam Donaldson happen to cross paths on the courthouse steps. Their familiarity has become so established that they casually raise their paper McDonald's coffee cups in salute to one another and share a casual, "Mornin' Sam,"… "Mornin' Squeaky".

Following up on that premise which we joke about in the previous paragraph, the reporters covering the story begin to note a pattern of comments that they've been hearing from their newfound friends, the Manson girls. Charlie's Angels have been making more frequent references to the notion that Charlie will soon be out. There is a collective observation noted by the reporters. They find it interesting that the girls never use the words released or acquitted. There is an underlying fear that some kind of a breakout plan is in the works.

On June 1, 1969, two weeks before the trial is to begin, Manson again requests a change of attorneys. The basis for this move on his part seems to be the ill-conceived notion that he can somehow reestablish himself as his own attorney. When Manson's motion is denied, he replies to the judge that his alternative is to cause him as much trouble as possible.

It won't take long for Manson to show his hand. During the court session of June 9, Charlie spontaneously swivels his chair so as to face his back toward the judge. At this point Manson says, "The Court has shown me no respect so I'm going to show the Court the same thing."[3] Judge Older subsequently makes multiple requests for Manson to respect the Court by facing the judge and after repeated refusals Judge Older has the bailiffs remove him from the courtroom.

Manson is then taken to an adjoining lockup from which he can view the proceedings but not participate in them. In that adjoining room Manson is extended multiple opportunities to rejoin the proceedings providing he can behave properly. Manson declines the offers.

At this point, what the trial clearly needs is a chime-in from Sexy Sadie. Susan Atkins (aka Sexy Sadie) rises and says, "If your Honor does not respect Mr. Manson's rights, you need not respect mine."[4]

Subsequently, Patricia Krenwinkel and Leslie Van Houten each stand, turn their backs to the judge, and repeat Susan Atkins' words.

Next, Judge Older suggests that the defense attorneys might intervene on behalf of their clients. Patricia Krenwinkel's attorney Paul Fitzgerald, while acknowledging the appropriateness of this suggestion, also notes the obvious flaw in the strategy by pointing out that "there is a minimum of client control in this case."[5] After repeated incidents of disruption, Judge Older comes to the determination that he has no choice but have the girls removed to a vacant upstairs jury room where they are provided with an audio feed of the proceedings.

Fitzgerald's comment above accentuates an odd but unavoidable observation regarding the trial. The judicial process must be upheld in this trial, as well as any other. That being said, it is clearly the goal of the defendants to disrupt the trial's process to the greatest degree possible. This overall scenario obviously forces Judge Older to walk a tight wire. He needs to strike that fine balance between showing some level of patience with the defendants, yet still maintaining a semblance of order in the court.

While understanding Older's need to maintain order, prosecuting defense attorney Bugliosi has mixed emotions about this turn of events. Depriving the defendants of their presence in the courtroom, as well as compromising their communications with their attorneys, are both developments that could theoretically be used as grounds to aid an appeal. Bugliosi urges Older to establish a line of telephone communication between the girls and their attorneys but that request is denied by the judge.

During the lunch break the girls express their desire to return to the courtroom. Speaking to Judge Older, Patricia Krenwinkel says, "We should be able to be present at this play here."[6] While doubtful that her double entendre is intentional, we can't help but focus on her use of the word "play." Think of the two basic meanings this word can have. It can mean #1) an entertaining performance of a story or #2) the fun playing of a game. Ironically to Krenwinkel, Atkins and Van Houten, these court proceedings are both.

As confirmation of our theory, here's what happens next. Upon being granted re-entry to the courtroom, but before the afternoon session even begins, Krenwinkel stands up and turns her back to the judge. Atkins and Van Houten immediately follow suit. Judge Older once again removes the girls, the circus atmosphere they have sought being thusly achieved.

The next morning Judge Older brings all the trial participants together to attempt a do-over. In a statement that can be acknowledged as both an admonishment and an advisement, the judge warns the girls that, "I would ask you to seriously reconsider what you are doing, because I think you are hurting yourselves."

This day's games will begin with Manson once again requesting the right to defend himself. Upon denial of that request, Manson says, "Okay, then you leave me nothing. You can kill me now."[7] Accentuating the drama, Manson assumes the outstretched-arm pose of a crucifixion. The girls fall in line with their leader's game of Simon Says and immediately assume the same pose. At that point the judge gets to play Simon and orders all four out of the courtroom.

All four defendants refuse to obey Simon's demand to vacate, necessitating their physical removal from the proceedings. Manson ends up wrestling with a deputy on the floor before being dragged out. Enhancing the charade, Manson's attorney Irving Kanarek requests medical assistance for his client. He is assured by the judge that if such assistance is needed, it will be provided. Turns out, Charlie is just fine.

JURY SELECTION BEGINS ~ The morning of Monday, June 15, 1970, sees the beginning of the jury selection process which, like most everything else in this trial, will become an event in and of itself. The first consideration of the judge in this regard will be whether or not to sequester the jury. In pondering this, the actual decision is certainly much easier than couching the public explanation so as not to seem prejudicial.

In dealing with the likes of the Manson Family, it is pretty much a no-brainer that the jury will need to be protected from the type of intimidation that is the general modus operandi of the cult. Judge Older rules that the jury will be sequestered, in his words to "protect them from harassment and to prevent their being exposed to trial publicity."[8]

Being selected to this jury is certainly not going to be a walk in the park. General estimates of the length of the trial range up to six months, some even higher. So all jurors will spend that entire time holed up in a hotel, denied all access to news and media, and allowed weekend-only visits from family members. And if you think about it, that may be the good part. Imagine life in the aftermath of being one of twelve jurors who votes to send Charles Manson to the gas chamber. How do you _not_ spend the rest of your life looking over your shoulder?

Shifting gears, from a terrified jury to a terrified judge, copied below is a secret memo that Judge Older had sent to the Los Angeles Sheriff's Office. Notice it's written more in the form of a demand than a request. Older's memo reads, "The LASO shall provide the trial judge with a driver-bodyguard, and security shall be provided at the trial judge's residence on a 24-hour basis, until such time as all pre- and post-trial proceedings have been concluded."[9] While Older's request is totally understandable, it does also serve to accentuate the danger of being involved with this trial.

We have one final thought to share before proceeding to the actual process of jury selection. The quote that ends this paragraph was one of our favorites from this book. Think about this and put it in the context of this trial. When someone is summoned for jury duty it's not like you get a heads-up on what you're walking into. When the first batch of prospective jurors walk into the courtroom and perfunctorily peruses the premises, a rancid reality resonates. "Oh, my God," exclaims one potential juror, "it's the Manson trial."[10]

CHAPTER 14:
LOTSAPOPPA AND MORE
(JUNE 16-JULY 24, 1970)

BUGLIOSI – MANSON CONVERSATION PIECE ~ On multiple occasions Manson attempts stare-down sessions with both Judge Older and Prosecuting Attorney Bugliosi as an attempt at intimidation. It is Bugliosi's theory that Manson had perfected these practices of concentration while in prison. While Older chooses to simply ignore Manson, Bugliosi opts for an alternate strategy, considering these stare-downs an opportunity to engage his adversary.

We are about to share some intriguing conversations between Vincent Bugliosi and Charles Manson which we need to preface with a very important nuance. Having spent half of his life in prison, Manson is enough of a jailhouse rat to know that legally, he can say anything to Bugliosi in a private conversation and his comments cannot be used against him in trial because he has not been advised of his rights.

Knowing that, let's listen in on some courtroom conversations. In the midst of one of their stare-downs, Bugliosi actually slides his chair adjacent to Charlie's and initiates the conversation we will outline below. It's one of a handful of conversations between Manson and Bugliosi that, by their nature, are rather striking. They are characterized by a let-the-chips-fall-where-they-may, Devil-may-care attitude; the latter of those two clichés being particularly apropos.

BUGLIOSI: Charlie? Are you afraid of me?
MANSON: You think I'm bad and I'm not.
BUGLIOSI: I don't think you're all bad, Charlie. For instance, I understand you love animals.
MANSON: Then you know I wouldn't hurt anyone.

BUGLIOSI: Hitler loved animals too, Charlie. He had a dog named
               Blondie, and from what I've read, Adolf was very kind to
               Blondie.[1]

Some folks compared Charlie to Hitler
Chuck sent out a hit girl to get her
Said Sharon, "Please save me,
I'm having a baby"
But rather than save her, she slit her.

There's another reason why the Bugliosi/Manson conversations are
so interesting. As we stated above, because they take place in the context
where Manson has not been read his rights, nothing he says can come up
in the trial or ever be used against him. Notice in this next conversation,
since Charlie is free to say anything, he freely admits to shooting a man
fully knowing that admission cannot come back to haunt him.

Switching subjects, Manson goes on to ask why Bugliosi thinks he is
responsible for these murders. Bugliosi points out that both Susan Atkins
and Linda Kasabian have told him that Charlie is responsible, and he
asks why the girls would say that if it wasn't true. Manson tells him the
girls are just trying to get attention and that he would never hurt anyone.

Bugliosi responds by saying, "Don't give me that crap, Charlie, because I
just won't buy it! What about Lotsapoppa? You put a bullet in his stomach."
Manson's response is, "Well, yeah, I shot the guy. He was going to come up
to Spahn Ranch and get all of us. That was kind of in self-defense."[2]

LOTSAPOPPA ~ Please allow us to diverge and share the story of
"Lotsapoppa". The nickname is an epithet which, in and of itself, makes the
tale worth telling. An epithet is a name or title which is descriptive of the person
that is being referred to. Here are a couple of examples to illustrate the concept:
Alexander the "Great", Michael "Air" Jordan, and "Chubby" Checker.

Lotsapoppa is a huge black dude with an overactive libido. He will
also serve as an asterisk to a go-to claim that Charles Manson would often
make later in his life. Coming to his own defense, and maintaining his
innocence Manson would routinely boast, "I never killed nobody."[3]

While that may have been true, there is a point in his life that Manson was sure he had killed someone.

Manson and Bernard Crowe (Lotsapoppa) get into a dispute over drugs and money (Surprise, surprise). Manson ends up shooting Crowe in the belly and in an attempt to save his life, Lotsapoppa pretends like he's Lotsa-dead. He almost was. After spending 18 days in intensive care, upon his release from the hospital, Crowe subsequently has his friends confirm his "death" to Manson in order to prevent Charlie from returning to take a second shot at it. In legendary Lotsapoppa lore, there are a couple more stories worth sharing.

Having put the bullet in the big guy himself, Manson has no reason to doubt the demise detailed by Lotsapoppa's friends. Upon Manson's arrest later in the story, fate orchestrates a rare reunion of reconciliation. Imagine Charlie's surprise when one day, walking down the halls of the L.A. courthouse, he finds himself face-to-face with a ghastly ghost from his ghoulish past.

Son of a bitch if it's not Lotsapoppa! Anxious to have things end on a positive note, Charlie offers an olive branch. However, Charlie's belated apology doesn't remove the bullet that's still in Lotsapoppa's belly. But perhaps surprisingly, by this point Lotsapoppa is actually indebted to Manson in a twisted kind of way which we'll explain next.

Vincent Bugliosi actually seeks out Lotsapoppa during the course of the investigation because of that bullet from the shooting which has never been removed. Bugliosi knows that the striations on that bullet could serve to more fully link Manson to the gun, which was the same one used in the Tate murders. Bugliosi tells Lotsapoppa that if he'd like to have the bullet removed, it would be paid for. Lotsapoppa politely declines. He views it as a badge of honor and talks about having the ultimate conversation starter at the local tavern!

The chicks seem to dig Lotsapoppa
The dude was the big enchilada
But things hit rock bottom
And then Manson shot him
Which made Chuck persona non grata

Culminating a process that took five weeks, both prosecution and defense agree to accept the jury on July 14. It is a mixed jury, diverse in age as well as gender. There are seven men and five women, ranging in age from 25 to 73. In analyzing their occupations, the one we find most uniquely connected to the trial is that of mortician. Others range from teachers to secretaries to road workers.

LAWYER CHEAT SHEET ~ With the trial imminently looming we will hereby provide for you, our devoted readers, a chart to use for handy reference in linking the defendants and their lawyers.

Charles Manson/Irving Kanarek (49, obnoxious, bombastic, prolongs trials)

Susan Atkins/Daye Shinn (40, seeks out Manson trial for celebrity opportunity)

Patricia Krenwinkel/Paul Fitzgerald (32, articulate, competent, most quoted)

Leslie Van Houten/Ronald Hughes (34, hippie vibe, inexperienced, disappears)

Of the four defense attorneys we will include applicable aspects of their personal stories as they relate to significant moments in the trial. Only one of the four warrants a full-fledged pre-trial discovery, that being Charles Manson's attorney, Irving Kanarek. To begin in layman's terms, the man was a royal pain in the ass which is exactly why Manson had chosen him.

He was known for his ability to paralyze trials through a variety of tactics. He was prone to incessant ramblings, outlandish charges and senseless motions. It was Bugliosi's intuition that Kanarek's strategy in the trial would be to draw it out for as long as possible by the exorbitant use of questionable legal tactics. Putting two and two together, having Kanarek as the attorney and the Manson crew as the defendants would make for the perfect storm. Kanarek could excruciatingly extend the trial allowing even more time for the defendants to create chaos in the courtroom in the hope that something might go so dreadfully wrong, a mistrial would be warranted.

Bugliosi was in fact so adamantly opposed to Kanarek's involvement that he actually made a motion to the court to have him taken off the case. From a common sense point of view, Bugliosi accurately pointed out that Kanarek's participation would cost the people of the State of California millions of dollars. From a legal perspective, Bugliosi's argument was that while Manson did have the right to choose his lawyer, that right is extended for the purpose of having the defendant choose the lawyer that is most able to secure a positive verdict for said defendant. In this case, Bugliosi argued, Manson was choosing a lawyer solely on the basis of who could most help him disrupt the trial, therefore the choice of Kanarek should be disallowed. Judge Older denied Bugliosi's motion and Kanarek would remain on the case.

Friday, July 24, is to be the first day of testimony. Before the first beams of sunlight begin to penetrate the Los Angeles skyline, a crowd has already begun to assemble outside the courtroom hoping to get a seat for the inevitable theatrics. The whole scene is just so surreal with the Manson Family prophets milling about the courtroom steps as if waiting for the Romans to put their Jesus Christ on trial.

Astute observers notice that the prophets are carrying flyers this morning. This obviously arouses curiosity, but it is a curiosity that will not be satisfied before the beginning of the trial. Until then, the prophets would keep a tight grip upon their flyers. What news might these documents decry?

The answer to this question will be revealed when Charles Manson is escorted into the courtroom. Upon seeing him, an audible gasp envelopes the room reflecting the collective response to two basic questions. #1) How had Manson been able to secure access to a sharp object overnight? #2) What is the symbolic meaning of the bloody "X" he has carved into the flesh on his forehead with that sharp object?

Connecting the dots, Manson's prophets spring into action, more than happy to answer question #2. They begin passing out their flyers to the overflow crowd of people who have come too late to secure a seat to witness the proceedings in person. But the circus atmosphere and bizarre air of adventure combine to create a situation where people don't want to leave. Thanks to Manson and, ironically reflective of his crimes, the street vendors are making a killing.

"X" MARKS THE SPOT ～ Regarding the flyer, as is often the case, Charlie tends to ramble a bit. We'll share with you the excerpted version.

Providing the background for his bloody brand, Manson proclaims, "I have X'd myself from the establishment's world. You have created the monster. I stand opposed to what you do and have done in the past. You make fun of God and have murdered the world in the name of Jesus Christ. My faith in me is stronger than anything you may want to do to me. Your courtroom is a man's game. Love is my judge."[4]

To summarize our feelings on the flyer, I guess we'd sarcastically say, "If you're going to walk into court with a bloody "X" carved into your forehead, it's always good to be able to offer a totally logical explanation as to why." Over the following weekend each of the female defendants replicate the "X", carving the symbol into their own foreheads, as did most of the other Manson Family members. Years later Manson embellished his symbol, modifying his "X" into a swastika. Ever the artist.

Chapter 15:
Opening Statement
(July 24-26, 1970)

BUGLIOSI'S OPENING STATEMENT ~ Proceedings begin with the bailiff stating the name of the case as "The People vs. Charles Manson, Susan Atkins, Patricia Krenwinkel and Leslie Van Houten". After that the baton is passed to Vincent Bugliosi for his opening statement. Bugliosi begins the statement as follows.

> "A question you ladies and gentlemen will probably ask yourselves at some point during this trial, and we expect the evidence to answer that question for you is this. What kind of a diabolical mind would contemplate or conceive of these seven murders? What kind of mind would want to have seven human beings brutally murdered?"

At this point, for the sake of concision we will excerpt what we see as the most important points in Bugliosi's lengthy opening statement. He continues...

> "Evidence at this trial will show defendant Charles Manson to be a vagrant wanderer, a frustrated singer-guitarist, a pseudo-philosopher, but, most of all, the evidence will conclusively prove that Charles Manson is a killer who clearly masqueraded behind the common image of a hippie."
>
> "The evidence will show that Manson was the unquestioned leader and overlord of a nomadic band of vagabonds who called themselves the 'Family'. We anticipate that Mr. Manson, in his defense, will claim that neither he nor anyone else was the leader of the

Family and that he never ordered anyone in the Family to do anything, much less commit these murders for him."

"We therefore intend to offer evidence at this trial showing that Charles Manson was in fact the diabolical leader of the Family; that everyone in the Family was slavishly obedient to him; that he always had the other members of the Family do his bidding for him; and that eventually they committed the seven Tate-LaBianca murders at his command."[1]

Bugliosi goes on to explain that the primary witness for the prosecution will be one Linda Kasabian. The fact that she was at both crime scenes puts her in an unique position to testify about the proceedings that took place both nights. She will be key in connecting the physical evidence the prosecution will present to the specifics of the crimes.

Up to this point Bugliosi's task has been pretty much standard procedure, if indeed such a phrase can be applied to any element of the horrific crimes for which these defendants are being tried. But the next part of his opening statement presents a challenge unlike anything he has faced before. Bugliosi is next charged with explaining what might well be truly the most bizarre motive in the annals of human crime.

EXPLAINING THE MOTIVE ~ Having read our book up to this point, our next challenge for you will be a difficult one because if you're still with us now you've been "Helter Skeltered" up the wazoo. But imagine you're sitting in the jury box with none of that background whatsoever. Even if you've been following the case in the news, the Helter Skelter motive has not been publically written about or discussed until this point. Talk about your "What in the World?" moment!

Addressing motive, Bugliosi says...

"We believe there to be more than one motive. Besides the motives of Manson's passion for violent death and his extreme anti-establishment state of mind, the evidence in this trial will show that there was a further motive for these murders, which is perhaps as bizarre, or perhaps even more bizarre, that the murders themselves.

"The evidence will show Manson's fanatical obsession with Helter Skelter, a term he got from the English musical group the Beatles. Manson was an avid follower of the Beatles and believed that they were speaking to him across the ocean in the lyrics to their songs."

"To Charles Manson, Helter Skelter, the title of one of their songs, meant the black man rising up and destroying the entire white race; that is, with the exception of Charles Manson and his chosen followers, who intended to escape from Helter Skelter by going to the desert and living in a bottomless pit, a place that Manson derived from Revelation 9, a chapter from the last book of the New Testament."

"Evidence from several witnesses will show that Charles Manson hated black people, but that he also hated the white establishment, whom he called 'pigs'. The word 'Pig' was found printed in blood on the outside of the front door of the Tate residence. The words 'Death to Pigs', 'Helter Skelter', and 'Rise' were found printed in blood inside the LaBianca residence. The evidence will show that one of Manson's principle motives for these seven savage murders was to ignite Helter Skelter; in other words, start the black-white revolution by making it look as though the black man had murdered these seven Caucasian victims."

"In his twisted mind he thought this would cause the white community to turn against the black community, ultimately leading to a civil war between blacks and whites, a war which Manson told his followers would see bloodbaths in the streets of every American city, a war which Manson predicted and foresaw the black man as winning."

"Manson envisioned that black people, once they destroyed the entire white race, would be unable to handle the reins of power because of inexperience, and would therefore have to turn over the reins to those white people who had escaped from Helter Skelter; i.e., Charles Manson and his Family. In Manson's mind, his Family, and particularly he, would be the ultimate beneficiaries of a black-white civil war."

"We intend to offer the testimony of not just one witness but many witnesses on Manson's philosophy, because the evidence will show that it is so strange and so bizarre that if you heard it from the lips of only one person you probably would not believe it."[2]

BACKGROUND ON THE CRIME ~ At this point, Bugliosi's target has been focused almost completely on Charles Manson, which is sound strategy because obviously he is the biggest fish to fry. But before completing his opening statement he will have to throw his net over the women as well.

Bugliosi goes on to highlight the savagery with which the murders were committed. Talk about your overkill; at the Tate residence Voytek Frykowski had been stabbed 51 times, absorbed 13 violent blows to the head, and been shot twice. At her house, Rosemary LaBianca was stabbed 41 times.

In terms of establishing the utter guilt of these co-defendants, Bugliosi can also point out one important additional fact. All the killings occur in scenarios where Charles Manson isn't even present. Bugliosi closes by sharing his confidence that the jury will give both the defendants and the People of the State of California the fair and impartial trial to which each is entitled.

During Bugliosi's opening statement, Irving Kanarek continues to display the disruptive tactics Bugliosi has expected. He objects nine times and upon the completion of Bugliosi's statement, Kanarek requests a mistrial. All of these antics are dismissed by Judge Older.

In a move that reminds us of the coin flip at the beginning of a football game, the defense, while having the option to deliver its opening statements at the beginning of the trial, defers to the second half. They choose to deliver their statements after the prosecution has rested its case. That sets things up for the first witness who is to be Colonel Paul Tate, Sharon's father.

COLONEL PAUL TATE ~ Tate's testimony is perfunctory. Probably the greatest drama of his appearance stems from the fact that it is rumored that he has vowed to kill Manson. Subsequently he is thoroughly searched before entering the courtroom and the bailiffs watch him closely throughout the proceedings, which are brief. Bugliosi has Tate identify pictures of his daughter, the other victims, and the house at 10050 Cielo Drive. The purpose of this first witness seems to be a humanistic one, creating sympathy for the victim. The dead Sharon Tate has left behind a grieving father.

WILFRED PARENT ~ The next witness is Wilfred Parent, the father of Steven Parent. On the night of the Tate murders, Steven is the unfortunate victim of being in the wrong place at the wrong time. He happens to be departing the Tate compound after visiting William Garretson, a friend who is living in the guest house on the property. Parent is pulling out of the driveway just as the Manson murder crew has entered the compound. Fearing Parent might have seen them, Tex Watson flags him down and shoots him dead. When shown a picture of his son, Wilfred Parent breaks down in tears.

WINIFRED CHAPMAN ~ Witness #3 is the maid at the Tate household, Winifred Chapman. Bugliosi's main purpose in calling the maid to the stand has to do with her cleaning responsibilities. Fingerprints linking two defendants to the crime scene had been found on doors at the Tate residence. Ms. Chapman confirms that both doors had been washed during the day of the murders Friday, August 8, subsequently eliminating any possibility that the prints might have been left over from any previous visits by the defendants.

WILLIAM GARRETSON ~ The next witness, William Garretson is the caretaker who was living in the guest house at the Tate residence. Garretson had been taken into custody after the murders and was the primary suspect in the first several hours after the crime was discovered. He was truly just a victim of location, happening to be on the grounds at the time.

The one thing about him that initially arouses suspicion is that the whole process characterizing the Tate murders was so chaotic you'd think he must have heard something. Garretson says he'd been listening to music and never heard anything. When asked how loud the volume was, he replies that, "It was about medium. Something like that. It wasn't very loud, you know. It was just enough so that I could hear it."[3] That, in and of itself, oddly makes him seem innocent. If he had been lying about not hearing anything, he probably would have also lied and said the music was really loud, just to cover his tracks.

By the end of the day on Friday, Bugliosi has questioned all of his preliminary witnesses and the stage is set. On Monday morning the prosecution will be introducing its primary witness Linda Kasabian. But the time between the end of the court session on Friday and Monday morning will not be uneventful.

Friday afternoon, while being escorted from the courtroom back to his jail cell, Manson tries to bribe the guard to release him. Manson's comments are made with somewhat abstract couched wording so as to avail himself of at least a thread of plausible deniability. For example Manson tells the guard that it would be worth $100,000 to him to be set free. He doesn't come right out and make a direct bribe, but he sets it out there clearly enough that the meaning is evident.

Always looking out for the best interests of his prison guards, Manson also mentions that the jail sentence for a guard who lets a prisoner go, without the proper authority, is just six months. If you put those two pieces together the question becomes, would you be willing to spend six months in jail for $100,000? The guard opts for Plan B and turns Manson in.

The girls also find engaging activities to warm up their weekend. Susan Atkins, Patricia Krenwinkel and Leslie Van Houten heat up bobby pins until they are red hot, then burn X's into their foreheads. After that they use needles to tear open the burnt flesh making the X's more prominent. After all, girls just wanna have fun.

CHAPTER 16:
STAR WITNESS
(JULY 27-AUGUST 3, 1970)

LINDA KASABIAN ~ Monday morning, after noticing that now all four defendants have become part of "Generation X", the court settles in for the testimony of Linda Kasabian. Bugliosi has her explain that she does understand that she is being granted immunity from prosecution in exchange for her cooperation in the trial. Next he has Kasabian explain the dynamics of the Manson Family lifestyle and the degree to which Charlie is in charge. Then Bugliosi has her explain Manson's Helter Skelter theory.

Methodically painting his picture, Bugliosi moves on to the crimes themselves. Kasabian relates the events of August 8, beginning in the afternoon when Manson announces it is time for Helter Skelter. She takes the jury on the ride from Spahn Ranch to 10050 Cielo Drive. Since the details have been provided previously we'll not repeat those, but suffice it to say Kasabian calmly and clearly clarifies all of the evening's events for the jurors.

Calamitously complicating that calmness and clarity, how's this for increasing her degree of difficulty? At one point during her testimony, when Kasabian happens to be passing a glance in Manson's general direction, Charlie smiles, takes his index finger and makes an ear-to-ear throat slashing gesture toward the witness stand.[1]

Giving up all the goods on their drug stash
Linda tells where they kept all their best hash
Not one to play nicely
Chuck gestures precisely
And tries to scare her with a throat slash

The next day the *LA Times* writes that "Linda Kasabian was surprisingly serene, soft-spoken, even demure."[2] The *Times* goes on to say that this was perhaps a juxtaposition of expectations on the levels of both the speaker and the topics about which she had to speak. Here on the stand was a participant in a mass murder speaking serenely and demurely about topics ranging from the killings to the group's sex life.

In writing our account of this story, it was our goal from the beginning to strive for the perfect balance between concision and depth. To that end we are choosing to employ some concision here. Manson's attorney Irving Kanarek, as previously established, is an obnoxious overbearing onerous obstructionist. As Bugliosi anticipates, Kanarek takes extreme measures to elongate and extend the trial by making constant motions and objections.

Here is our greatest example of this concept based upon the complete transcript of the trial we were able to review. At the moment, just before Judge Older calls the attorneys to the bench in the following paragraphs, there are literally twelve pages of transcript separating a Bugliosi question from Kasabian's answer to that question. These dozen pages all consist of courtroom banter necessitated by Kanarek's antics.

By the third day of the trial, when the number of Kanarek's objections has exceeded 200, Judge Older finally feels that the grounds have been established for him to intervene for the sake of the integrity of the trial. Upon calling Kanarek to the bench, Older cites him for contempt of court for the first time.

During the trial, Kanarek will be found guilty of contempt on four separate occasions. This first one comes when Judge Older finds Kanarek guilty of "directly violating my order not to repeatedly interrupt."[4] On two of the four contempt citings, Kanarek earns free overnight accommodations in the L.A. County Jail. At one point Older goes so far as to brand Kanarek as "totally without scruples, ethics, and professional responsibility."[5] And that's the judge speaking!

TUESDAY MORNING ~ Having covered the Tate murders in court on Monday, it is time for Bugliosi and Kasabian to move on to the LaBianca murders. Keep in mind, while Linda Kasabian had been present at the LaBianca home where Manson dropped off Tex Watson,

Susan Atkins, and Leslie Van Houten; Kasabian is driving the car which leaves that crime scene with Charles Manson, Steve "Clem" Grogan, and Patricia Krenwinkel.

Bugliosi's questions about the events of that evening focus upon a central theme which is to clearly establish Manson as being the driving force behind all of the group's actions and decisions. Upon close review of our transcript, the following is what we consider to be the most significant exchange.

BUGLIOSI: Did you ever see or observe any members of the Family refuse to do anything that Manson told him or her to do?

KASABIAN: No, nobody did. We always wanted to do anything and everything for him.[6]

At this point a very interesting exchange takes place between witness and defendant. These lines do not appear in the transcript, but for the sake of clout and continuity we'll revert to the format above for the exchange. Realizing he's on the ropes, Charlie starts the exchange with Linda in an off-hand comment which again, while never part of the official transcript, was clearly audible in the courtroom.

MANSON: *(as Linda walks by the defense table)* You've already told three lies.

KASABIAN: *(looking directly at him)* Oh no, Charlie, I've spoken the truth and you know it.

To quote Vincent Bugliosi, "By the time I had finished my direct examination of Linda Kasabian on the afternoon of July 30, I had the feeling that the jury knew it too."[7]

> *Telling the truth just to show it*
> *Making damn sure not to blow it*
> *Linda says to Chuck's face*
> *Putting him in his place,*
> *"I've spoken the truth and you know it"*

For Linda Kasabian this has been the relatively easy part. Coming up next will be the cross examination from not just one, but four different attorneys each looking to poke holes in her story.

The first attorney to cross exam Linda Kasabian is Paul Fitzgerald, Krenwinkel's attorney, whose basic strategy seems to be an attempt to compromise her credibility with a line of questioning emphasizing the pervasive lifestyle of the Family at the ranch. There are lots of questions about sex and drugs and Charlie worship. Kasabian answers calmly and honestly, not allowing Fitzgerald to rattle her or really score any points at all for his client.

Susan Atkins' attorney Daye Shinn is up next and he takes the strategy of trying to make it look like Kasabian had been coached in her testimony by Vincent Bugliosi. Kasabian does a good job of indicating that is not the case. Shinn is subsequently also deprived of scoring anything that might be qualified as a victory.

On the day that Kasabian's cross examination by Irving Kanarek is to begin, a new star unexpectedly emerges as the centerpiece of the trial. How can such a thing occur in midtrial and who might that party crashing star be? As fate would have it, on August 3, 1970, the most significant person in the trial will become none other than President Richard Nixon.

In retrospect, when reflecting upon his impeachment, we all usually focus on Watergate. But, truth be told, Nixon's inability to get out of his own way is also evidenced in many other adventures we tend to forget. Here's our case in point regarding the Manson trial.

At a conference of law enforcement officials in Denver, Nixon is complaining about the press saying they "glorify and make heroes out of those engaged in criminal activities."[8] Nixon continues, saying "I noted, for example, the coverage of the Charles Manson case is front page every day in the papers. It usually gets a couple of minutes in the evening news. Here's a man who is guilty, directly or indirectly, of eight murders. Yet here's a man who, as far as the coverage is concerned, appears to be a glamorous figure."[9]

Well, now that the President of the United States has already rendered a verdict in this trial, can't we just let the judge and jury go home and have the defendants find their place in the line for the gas chamber? It's hard not to draw parallels between this press bashing and modern-day politics. In Presidents past and present we see concerning examples of a concept called the "Cobra Effect."

Our concise definition of the Cobra Effect is, "When an attempted solution to a problem unintentionally results in making the problem worse, as a type of unintended consequence." The term is often used to describe unwanted political results. Nixon's 1969 attack on the press was intended to vilify Manson but it actually had the potential the most beneficial thing that happened to Charlie during the trial.

Please allow us to don our turbans and snake charming garb to sway back and forth and lure the Cobra Effect out of its basket. By the way, if the concept of the Cobra Effect has captured your fancy, we have actually written a separate article on this topic which we will include as one of our appendices to this book for those of you who would enjoy a more thorough examination.

Why does Nixon's statement qualify as an example of the Cobra Effect? Richard Nixon makes his accusatory remarks in hopes of hurting Manson. Is Nixon able to damage Manson's case? No. Instead his judgments of Manson actually lay the groundwork for the defense's best chance ever to petition for a mistrial. Note to Richard: You've just been bitten by the Cobra Effect.

In the aftermath of the ill-advised comment by Nixon, damage control is begun by his presidential press secretary Ron Ziegler who says Nixon "failed to use the word 'alleged'" in referring to the charges. "The phrase he used could lead to some misinterpretation,"[10] Ziegler added. As we see is still the case today, lame excuses by presidential press secretaries are not always able to atone for the tirades from the top.

While in the air, flying back to Washington on Air Force One, Nixon subsequently tries to walk back the mistake issuing the following statement. "I have been informed that my comment in Denver regarding the Tate murder trial in Los Angeles may continue to be misunderstood despite the unequivocal statement made by my press secretary. The last thing I would do is prejudice the legal rights of any person, in any circumstances."

"To set the record straight," Nixon said in his statement at Andrews Air Force Base, "I do not know and did not intend to speculate as to whether the Tate defendants are guilty, in fact, or not. All the facts in the case have not been presented. The defendants should be presumed to be innocent at this stage of the trial."[11]

Nixon's comments create the need for a significant effort on the part of the court and the police to clean up the mess created by the President. Judge Older summons all the attorneys to his chambers. At the point in time when the news breaks, the jurors have already returned from lunch and are currently sequestered in a conference room. There is no way any of them could have been exposed to the news at this stage of the game.

There is a discussion as to what appropriate measures shall be taken to deal with the situation. What are they to do? Well, Kanarek immediately, and predictably, calls for a mistrial, which of course is denied. The bailiffs are instructed to scour the courtroom and remove any newspapers. Then planning begins on the preventative measures needed to be taken when the jurors leave the courthouse.

The windows on the bus which would take them back to their hotel need to be covered to prevent them from seeing the inevitable headlines which could be visible on sidewalk newsstands. At the Ambassador Hotel, where the jurors are staying, they have a joint recreation room which does have a television.

The usual rules regarding watching the TV are that the jurors can watch any shows they want, except for the news. Changing of channels can only be done by the bailiffs. On this particular night, to protect from the possibility of a newsflash regarding Nixon's gaffe spontaneously scrolling across the screen, the TV goes black.

Exactly how Charles Manson learns the news is not clear, but his face is beaming and his eyes are aglow when all the involved parties return from the lunch break. Manson's list of already-achieved take downs includes movie stars and millionaires; now he can add the President of the United States to that list.

CHAPTER 17:
LINDA KASABIAN
CONTINUES THE GOOD FIGHT
(AUGUST 3, 1970-AUGUST 13, 1970)

Finally, Irving Kanarek takes his shot at questioning Linda Kasabian and he does have some success. He is able to point out that when Kasabian came back to California to be reunited with her daughter, she made a mistake in the paperwork she had been required to complete. She had indicated her date of departure from California as August 6. Obviously if that had been true, it would have been ultimately significant because it would have meant she would not have been able to be present at either of the crime scenes about which she has testified.

While this mistake may make her look careless or disorganized, it probably does little damage to how the jurors assess her credibility. She had actually left on August 13, so she is off by exactly one week. Maybe she glanced at a calendar, remembered it was a Wednesday and just picked the wrong day; or maybe, anxious to see her daughter Tanya again, she was just careless.

Either way, she truly is in L.A. on the days of the murders and there are witnesses who can corroborate that fact. Even if Manson could orchestra a Family fabrication regarding the whereabouts of Kasabian, prosecution witness Barbara Hoyt would be able to corroborate Kasabian's presence at the Spahn Ranch when the Family was watching the newscast about the Tate murders.

In what will turn out to be the cross examination from Hell, Kanarek keeps Kasabian on the witness stand for seven days. We'll spare you almost all of the excruciating details and pick out just a couple of spots that seem most significant.

Kasabian testifies that her mind is clear on the evening of the Tate murders. There is a consensus to this truth. Everyone in the Manson

Family involved on either of the nights in question concurs on that. Manson's use of drugs, as well as the drug use by his Family, is keenly calculated. Charlie carefully considers his planned agenda before doling out the drugs. His words to live by are...

> *If there's an orgy on the docket*
> *Take the acid from your pocket*
> *If murders are the fate tonight*
> *I need you people straight tonight*

At any rate, let's proceed with our story working on the premise that there has been no drug intake on Kasabian's part, nor any other member of the Manson Family, during the evening of the Tate murders. In questioning her, Kanarek also extracts the comment that, after seeing Tex Watson shoot Steven Parent, Kasabian goes into a state of shock. Now on one level, you can possibly take those two pieces of information and see them as contradictory. Kanarek's point is, how can someone be totally cognizant and also in a state of shock?

If one is truly in a state of shock could it be accurate to say one's mind is clear? And while we must acknowledge some sense of validity to that contradiction, it's really just a game of semantics. As Bugliosi points out upon his follow-up questioning of Kasabian, there's clearly a difference between being in a medically diagnosed "state of shock" versus being in a "state of shock" on an emotional level from having just witnessed a turbulent event.

The bottom line is that her testimony about the events of that evening are absolutely not blurred by any drugs. And how could any impressionable twenty-year-old girl not be shocked by seeing someone murdered in cold blood right in front of her?

So upon full consideration, the issue addressed in the paragraph above has absolutely no bearing on the guilt or innocence of the defendants, nor the truthfulness of Kasabian's testimony. In a trial where Kanarek knows his client is guilty as sin, it's merely an effort to obstruct and distract.

Next we'll document what seems to be Irving Kanarek's biggest misstep in his cross examination of Linda Kasabian. At one point his body language clearly changes, conveying that he is shifting gears. Kanarek goes to his table and returns with an envelope saying, "Mrs. Kasabian, I show you this picture."[1]

Upon seeing the photo Kasabian turns away and gasps, "Oh, God!"[2] It is the crime scene photo of Sharon Tate. Starkly screaming in bloody technicolor, the picture shockingly shows Sharon extremely dead and extremely pregnant. Noticing how shaken Kasabian is, Judge Older orders a ten-minute recess. Upon resuming the trial Kanarek proceeds to show Kasabian the crime scene photos of all the victims.

His presumed goal in this ploy is to perhaps rattle Kasabian into some kind of mistake. That goal, however, is not realized. Her sensitively emotional responses to Kanarek's shocking strategy actually seems to have an opposite effect upon the jury from what is intended. The witness who he has attempted to link to these heinous crimes is actually distanced from them.

At this point, it's three (lawyers) down and one to go for Linda Kasabian. The final defense attorney Kasabian will have to face would be Susan Atkins' attorney, Ronald Hughes. Even though he is the least experienced, Hughes may have done the most effective job in cross examination.

Working for him is the fact that, as Susan Atkins says, "Hughes was a big, bearded, long haired good-natured man. With a reputation as a 'hippie lawyer'."[3] Hughes uses his hippie background to establish a bit of a connection to Kasabian's experience with the Family enabling him to present to the jury a picture conveying the notion that essentially "this chick is too far out to be believed."

Hughes is able to extract from her that during her time with the Family she did a lot of drugs, thought Manson was Christ, and at times she felt she was a witch. He was able to combine these three pieces of information into a dramatic and effectively theatrical closing. Below, from the original transcript, are the final seven lines of the Ronald Hughes / Linda Kasabian testimony.

HUGHES:	You have testified that you have had trips on marijuana, hash, THC, morning-glory seeds, psilocybin, LSD, mescaline, peyote, methedrine, and Romilar, is that right?
KASABIAN:	Yes.
HUGHES:	And in the last year you have had the following major delusions: You have believed that Charles Manson is Jesus Christ, is that right?
KASABIAN:	Yes.
HUGHES:	And you believed yourself to be a witch?
KASABIAN:	Yes.
HUGHES:	Your Honor, I have no further questions at this time.[4]

So in conclusion, we do feel that Hughes' finish is effective in establishing Kasabian's quirkiness. But quirkiness notwithstanding, he doesn't really compromise her credibility. By this point Kasabian has been on the witness stand for 17 days and has done as good a job as the prosecution could have hoped for.

In terms of the jury believing Linda Kasabian, she is at one point handed a nice assist by Judge Older. Upon receiving a motion from the defense that Kasabian be examined by a court appointed psychiatrist, Older responds as follows. "I find no basis for a psychiatric examination in this case. She appears to be perfectly lucid and articulate. I find no evidence of aberration of any kind insofar as her ability to recall, to relate. In all respects she has been remarkably articulate and responsive. The motion will be denied."[5] After that testimonial, the defense has to be wishing it had never made the motion in the first place.

We have one more dramatic moment for Linda Kasabian before we will allow her to return home to New Hampshire and be reunited with her two children. On August 11, in the courtroom, Manson gives a long hand written letter to Kasabian. Upon first inspection it appears to be mostly gibberish, but after closer inspection Manson's words are freckled with small check marks. Upon excerpting the words between the check marks, the following coded message is revealed.

"Just give yourself to your love & give your love to be free. If you were not saying what you're saying there would be no trial. Don't use your love, it's only there for you. Why do you think they killed JC? Answer: Cause he was a Devil & bad. No one liked him. Don't let anyone have this or they will find a way to use it against me. This trial of Man's Son will only show the world that each man judges himself."[6]

Here's our analysis of Manson's strategy with this. It is a thinly veiled attempt to lure her back into the fold. With Kasabian having completed her testimony relatively unscathed, Manson is probably beginning to see the writing on the wall. Realistically, his best hope at this point would be that, after receiving her non-rescindable grant of immunity, Kasabian could repudiate her testimony and return to the Family. Or, as Kasabian did, she could just hand the letter to her lawyer.

Before returning to the Nixon debacle please allow us to finish the Linda Kasabian storyline. When Linda Kasabian concludes her testimony on August 10, 1970, the People of California, as per their agreement, petition the judge for her immunity from prosecution, and subsequent release. Judge Older signs the petition that same day, and Linda Kasabian is released on August 13, 1970.

What the hell, since we're going back to the hippie era anyway, right now, as we are prone to do, we're going to throw some funky karma your way. Check this out. Allow your eyeballs to scan upward and accurately absorb the actual August dates ascribed above. The August 10 date of the petition signing is the one-year anniversary of the LaBianca murders and the August 13 date of the release is the one-year anniversary of Kasabian escaping the Manson compound in California. How's that for some inspirational irony?

CHAPTER 18:
TIT FOR TAT EXCHANGES
(AUGUST 3-SEPTEMBER 11, 1970)

Another incident punctuates this eventful day when Kanarek continues his cross examination of Kasabian. Remember, earlier this same day the Richard Nixon brouhaha had brazenly broken. Well, the slick shtick of Tricky Dick has not come full circle yet.

Manson has a plan to take advantage of the fact that Nixon has, shortsightedly, publicly declared him guilty. Through his lawyers, Manson released the following statement. "Here's a man who is accused of murdering hundreds of thousands in Vietnam, who is accusing me of being guilty of eight murders."[1] Touché.

It is a bit of a challenge to figure out who the biggest dick is in this tit-for-tat exchange. And isn't that an interesting little colloquialism? One can't help but ponder the questions... What exactly is tat?... Where do I get some?... And how do I turn it in for the other thing?

Okay at this point we're feeling like it's time for you the readers and us the writers to collectively rein ourselves in, ~~get our tits together~~, er we mean ~~get our shit together~~, er how about we all just agree to refocus and collect our thoughts? Let's get back to the Nixon thing.

After stupidly stumbling into the statement stipulating Manson's guilt, the President makes headlines. At the lunchtime meeting initiated by Judge Older, courtroom bailiffs are instructed to scour the room being sure to remove any newspapers. While they certainly must have given that task their best effort, prepare yourself for some colorful courtroom theatrics from your favorite thespian, Charmin' Charlie.

That courtroom resumption begins with Irving Kanarek questioning Linda Kasabian. Shortly into this testimony, Charles Manson abruptly stands up, faces the jury, and holds up the front page of the *LA Times* emboldened with a supersized headline of, "MANSON GUILTY,

NIXON DECLARES". Bailiffs confiscate the paper as quickly as possible but the damage is done and the jurors are, for the first time, individually sequestered. This is done so that Judge Older can assess the effect of their exposure to the newspaper headline on an individual basis. Once again Charlie has succeeded in creating havoc.

Subsequent interviews by the judge determine most of the jurors had seen and read the headline. Once again let's gather everybody together in the judge's chambers to figure out what the hell we're going to do with this mess. Assuming you've been with us all along on this project, you can probably already predict the first thing that's going to happen. Manson's attorney Irving Kanarek calls for a mistrial. Mistrial denied.

Judge Older makes the determination that actually none of the jurors have been significantly influenced by the paper. A general consensus of the jury, expressed on an individual basis, is that they know a lot more about the trial than Nixon does. They have personally heard all of the testimony while Dick Nixon hasn't heard a word. Why the hell would they be swayed by any of Dick's drivel?

In Denver intending to suck up
To cops, Dick called Manson a fuck up
Of course it backfires
And as with most liars
Retirement for Nixon soon snuck up

BACK TO THE TRIAL ~ Meanwhile back at the trial, the second half of August, after Linda Kasabian's departure, is actually a bit anticlimactic. There is a three-day break for the State Bar Convention. Then the testimony that does occur is mostly focused upon scientific analysis of knives, guns, fingerprints and blood types.

Just as a sidebar, as we stated before, our goal in writing this book was not to have it be the definitive reference book on this topic. You can find that elsewhere. Our foremost goal was to have it be an engagingly entertaining read and, to that end, our strategy has been to strike the right balance between thoroughness and entertainment. If we found our research on a certain part of the trial to be boring, we chose not to pass that boredom onto you. We'll tell you what you need to know and move on quickly to the good stuff.

Speaking of moving on quickly, that's also what we're going to do with the first week of September. On the opening days of that month Bugliosi's primary witnesses are the police who discovered the various crime scenes. For the jury who has not yet been informed about these discoveries, it's important information. For our readers who've been with us from the beginning, you've had the murder scenes described to you already, so we're not going to repeat those descriptions.

THOMAS WALLEMAN ~ Let's pick things up again on September 7, when Bugliosi calls to the stand one Thomas Walleman. The goal with Walleman is to have him help link the gun known to be the Tate murder weapon to Manson. Walleman is in a position to contribute to this effort because he had accompanied Manson during the shooting of Bernard Crowe, or as we've come to know and love him, Lotsapoppa. During that incident, Walleman had actually handled the gun for a period of time, so Bugliosi is hoping Walleman can ID the weapon.

This testimony is by no means a slam dunk victory for Bugliosi. While acknowledging significant similarities, Walleman stops short of a definitive identification. A difficult thread connecting multiple witnesses called to the stand by Bugliosi is that obviously they are testifying with the fear of Manson retribution in the back of their minds which likely seems to be the case here.

BARBARA HOYT ~ Apply that concept to our next witness account. Barbara Hoyt is the young and pretty 17-year old who joins the Family in April of 1969. She may not have stayed with them all that long, but boy does she get her money's worth!

On the night of the Tate murders, upon being instructed by Susan Atkins, Hoyt grabs three sets of dark clothing from the Family's garment pile. Returning later with the clothes, she runs into Manson who tells her that Atkins and company have already left. Hoyt becomes suspicious the next night upon seeing Family members watching the news and becoming giddy at the sight of the Tate murder coverage.

Her fears that she's come to roost amongst a menagerie of maniacal murderers are confirmed the next week when she is awakened in the middle of the night by the screams of Donald "Shorty" Shea as he is being murdered. This killing has been ordered by Manson because Charlie suspects Shorty is responsible for providing the authorities with the information which led to the raid on August 16 at Spahn Ranch.

After hearing Susan Atkins admit to Family member Ruth Ann Moorehouse that she had killed Sharon Tate, Barbara Hoyt makes the determination that it is time to check out. Shortly thereafter, Hoyt flees the Family along with her friend Sherry Cooper. Defections just ruin Charlie's day so he seeks to retrieve them. Upon tracking them down in a diner, Charlie gives them money hoping to entice them to return to the fold. After the girls decline his offer, Charlie eventually finds himself eventually having to resort to Plan B. Trust us; it's a real trip.

When the trial begins Bugliosi contacts Hoyt and she reluctantly agrees to testify against Manson and his co-defendants. Seeing Hoyt's name on the witness list is cause for the Family members on the outside to spring into action. On September 5, Manson girls Squeaky Fromme and Ruth Ann Moorehouse contact Barbara Hoyt with an offer that sounds like it might have come from *Wheel of Fortune*. If Hoyt is willing to forego testifying, she will "win" a free all-expense-paid vacation to Hawaii.

Okay, we get it; Hoyt is still just 17 years old, innocent, impressionable and impulsive. But really, how does anyone not see some red flags going up at this point? Isn't it truly clear that this vacation is not going to end well? All of that being said, the way this flag gets run up the wrong pole will absolutely amaze you.

After signing on for this calamity, Barbara Hoyt spends the night of September 8 at Spahn Ranch. The next morning, she is driven by the Family to the airport where two tickets are purchased for Hoyt and Ruth Ann Moorehouse to fly to Hawaii. As vacation enhancements, each of the two girls are provided with $50 in cash and a stolen credit card. Regarding the credit cards, the irony can't get much better than this; one of them is a "TWA Getaway" card.

After checking into the Hilton Hawaiian Village Hotel, the typical enticements of a holiday vacation fall a bit short of Hoyt's expectations. Because of fear that they will be recognized by the police, Moorehouse requires that they remain holed up in the hotel. But one positive of the scenario is that Barbara and Ruth Ann, who had formerly been tight, are able to share some quality conversation time.

But as you might suspect, the girl talk is more manipulative than benevolent. Moorehouse tells Hoyt that Helter Skelter is inevitable and it would be in her best interest to accept that and come back to the Family. All of this is a clearly contrived effort to convince Hoyt to return to the fold, but she does not appear to be buying into it.

As Moorehouse realizes her most Family-friendly plan is failing, she falls back on a final option. It's the option of intimidation. As their "girl talk" continues Moorehouse shares a thinly veiled threat. She tells Hoyt that Linda Kasabian has less than six months to live. Whether that murder threat is missed by Hoyt, or it just didn't matter, is unclear.

Either way, it becomes obvious to Moorehouse that Barbara Hoyt is not going to be coaxed back to the Dark Side, a film reference that, although applicable, would not become a part of pop culture lexicon until later in the decade. During their Hilton Hawaiian Village Hotel hideout, Moorehouse does venture out once a day to make a long-distance phone call to a pay phone in L.A. which is being monitored by Lynette "Squeaky" Fromme.

When we first started researching this project, we never would have thought she had it in her, but in Manson's absence, Squeaky has become the unofficial head of the Family. Upon Moorehouse's returning from the phone call of September 9, Hoyt notices a distinct change in her demeanor. Hoyt is informed that Moorehouse will be flying home but she will be staying. The pair plan to hit the airport McDonald's for lunch before Moorehouse takes a 1:15 flight back to Los Angeles.

After receiving their burger order, Moorehouse takes the food back to the terminal waiting area, leaving Hoyt inside to pay. Upon reuniting the two gal pals enjoy their "two all-beef patties, special sauce, lettuce, cheese, pickles, onions, on a sesame seed bun" as the advertising catch phrase went at the time.

So at this point Barbara Hoyt is thinking that she's about to settle into a mundane McDonald's meal. But just when you think that you've been gypped, the bearded lady comes and does a double back flip.

Shortly before Moorehouse's departure, Hoyt hears the following cryptic line. Moorehouse says, "Imagine what it would be like if that hamburger had 10 hits of acid in it."[2] As the acid kicks in, the departing planes Hoyt sees through the airport windows, begin to look like pollen-laden bees buzzing off from their flowers as a surreal psychedelic reality suddenly sinks in. This is not the "special sauce" Hoyt had hoped for.

As Moorehouse leaves to board her plane, Hoyt continues to feel the effects of a massive acid overdose. Suddenly realizing she has become the victim of a murder attempt by her former Family, she panics, runs, and finally collapses.

Ironically, she is first discovered by a social worker with a background in drug treatment, allowing for her symptoms to be quickly diagnosed. She is rushed to the hospital for emergency treatment enhancing her recovery. The last thing she says, prior to passing out, shocks every doctor and nurse in the treatment room. Hoyt manages to utter the words, "Call Mr. Bugliosi and tell him I won't be able to testify today in the Sharon Tate trial."[3] A surreal silence saturates the surroundings.

That fast-food idea was boss
But condiments come with a cost
Those two all-beef patties
To which she would add cheese
Were fine, but please no "special sauce"

COMING DOWN OFF THE TRIP ~ Okay folks, it's time to return to the trial. We took a brief vacation for chronological reasons. In between the testimony of Thomas Walleman and Danny DeCarlo we needed to sidetrack to the saga of the Family's abduction of Barbara Hoyt. However, let's head home from Hoyt's hallucinogenic Hawaiian holiday hiatus and cue up our next witness.

While we are playfully alliterating allow us to share the following fun fact. If you love double D's, and let's face it who doesn't, this next sentence will be your favorite of the book. Because of the dynamic dimensions of his demonstrative dick, the Manson girls referred to Danny DeCarlo as Donkey Dan.

DANNY DECARLO ~ Danny DeCarlo's role within the Manson Family is definitely unique. His involvement with the Family stems from his membership in the "Straight Satans"[4] motorcycle gang. Demonstrating an admirably diverse flair for responsibility, DeCarlo is an officer in each group. He is the Treasurer for the Straight Satans and assumes the role of Sergeant at Arms for the Family.

Here's the explanation for how the paths of these two groups cross. The Straight Satans are a hell-raising L.A. motorcycle gang, notorious for a legendary lack of respect for the law. Collectively, they are Charlie's type of guys. Manson seeks a mutually symbiotic relationship where he will offer female favors for powerful protection. While the two groups dabble with the deal, it eventually falls apart and the Mansons and the Satans opt to take two different Highways to Hell. (Note: We had to get at least one AC⚡DC reference into this book somewhere and this seems like our best opportunity.)

Despite the departure of his cycle gang, Danny DeCarlo gets off on the girls and loves the laidback lifestyle so he stays. The fact that DeCarlo has always been into guns provides the perfect niche for him within the Family operation. For obvious reasons Manson has stockpiled an arsenal of weapons which he needs to keep finely tuned. An arrangement is made whereby every time DeCarlo would fix one of Manson's guns, Charlie would return a favor. Manson would provide a female outlet into which Danny could fire off his personal gun. It is a match made in Heaven.

But hearken the heavenly hazards hovering on the horizon. While the girls and the guns serve to cement a solid bond between Manson and Donkey Dan, Danny DeCarlo is never a head-over-heels, dyed-in-the-wool devoted disciple of Charles Manson. While hearing Helter Skelter, DeCarlo never really buys into the babbling biblical bullshit. For him, the bountiful buxom babes are more important than the Beatles and the Bible.

When the shit hits the fan and Manson goes down on a murder rap, Danny DeCarlo will not be one of the dudes on the courthouse steps flaunting flowers in his hair and carving crosses in his forehead. Quite the contrary, DeCarlo leaves the Family after the Shorty Shea murder and when push comes to shove, he cooperates fully with the police investigation.

DeCarlo is much less susceptible to Manson's intimidation for obvious reasons. When it comes to betting on that game of intimidation, DeCarlo will put his money on the Straight Satans over Charlie's Angels any day. But allow us to add one caveat just to assure that we don't sell Charlie short in terms of the fear he could instill.

On November 19, 1969, DeCarlo had agreed to lead Bugliosi and the LAPD on a guided tour of the Spahn Ranch where he would share all of the inside secrets that he knew. He agreed to lead the police tour on just one condition... he wanted the police to handcuff him, so any Family members who might witness the entourage will think that DeCarlo was only cooperating under duress.[5]

On September 11, 1970, Danny DeCarlo takes the witness stand. Prior to our sharing his testimony with you, allow us to pass on one sidebar. At this point, all the people who actually participated in the Tate-LaBianca murders are either in the courtroom (Manson, Atkins, Krenwinkel, Van Houten), or had been in it (Kasabian), except one. That solitary exception would be Charles "Tex" Watson who manages to fall back on some family favors to avoid extradition from Texas.

Other than the inconvenience of necessitating an additional trial for Watson, there is a second aspect of his absence that concerns Bugliosi. With Tex out of the picture, so to speak, it offers the defense a strategic opportunity to paint Tex as the bad guy. Might as well let him take the fall since he's not even there, right?

Contributing to the attractiveness of that strategy is the fact that you could honestly argue that, what the hell, Charlie isn't even at the scene of the crimes. Tex is clearly there and Tex is clearly the muscle behind the operation. So Bugliosi's primary goal with the testimony of DeCarlo is to extract from him a firsthand documentation of the nature of the relationship between Charles Manson and Tex Watson.

Bugliosi's questioning of DeCarlo basically accomplishes his goal, initially beginning with the character assessment of Tex Watson. About him DeCarlo says, "Tex was happy-go-lucky. He was a nice guy. I liked Tex. He didn't have no temper or anything I could see. He never said much."[6]

With those words DeCarlo seems to defuse the portrait of Tex Watson as a strong and violent crime leader. Furthermore, DeCarlo clearly defines the relationship between Manson and Watson. DeCarlo conveyed that Manson was the master of the Family and if Charlie told Tex to jump, Tex would ask, "How high?" DeCarlo said that Manson, "masqueraded as the 'devil'. Manson said he was the devil and the devil was on the loose."[7]

CHAPTER 19:
LEAPS OF FAITH
(SEPTEMBER 11-OCTOBER 5, 1970)

TEX WATSON ~ From the time of his arrest, it would be nine months before Tex Watson would leave his cell in Texas to bask in the warm California sun. It would not exactly be the return he'd hoped for. Going back to Manson's days when he was hanging out with the Beach Boys, maybe Charlie and Dennis Wilson could have saluted Tex Watson's California return by collaborating on a rewrite of the Beach Boys' summer anthem "Fun, Fun, Fun" that could've gone something like this…

> (to the tune of "Fun, Fun, Fun" by the Beach Boys)
> *Well Tex got in Charlie's car*
> *Grabbed the girls and went out Dirty Dancin'*
> *Tried to forget all about the seven murders*
> *That they just did for Manson*
> *But when it comes to goin' free*
> *You don't have a single bit of a chance, son*
> *And you'll be done, done, done*
> *When the jury takes your freedom away*

Well, we sure hope you're having as much fun, fun, fun as we are, so let's roll down the top, drive back to the trial, and pick up the Tex Watson storyline.

LEGAL BATTLE ~ One of the challenges of being a defense attorney in a trial where there are four defendants is that your client can be victimized by the decision of multiple other clients' lawyers. After Tex Watson returns to California, Patricia Krenwinkel's attorney Paul

Fitzgerald thinks it would be a good idea to call him into the courtroom in order to require Danny DeCarlo to make a positive ID.

Despite the strong objections of the other defense lawyers: Irving Kanarek (Manson), Daye Shinn (Atkins), and Ronald Hughes (Van Houten), Judge Older allows Fitzgerald's motion to bring Watson into the courtroom. Watson's appearance turns out to be a devastating blow to the defense team collectively. Here's why.

Up until this point the only image the jury has of Tex Watson is a literally drug-crazed mug shot taken in April of 1969. In that photo he certainly looks the part of a madman murderer. In the time since then, Watson has cleaned up, literally as well as figuratively. He's also lost 30 pounds and he looks five years younger than his actual age of 25.

When Watson walks into the courtroom dressed up in a coat and tie, with short well-trimmed hair, he looks like a preppy college kid. He makes his entry during the lunch break. The jury is still out so they do not see him walk in, but the defendants are already in place. Watson does not make eye contact with Manson but he does glance at the girls who swoon and blow kisses his way, prompting a reciprocatory grin. It makes for a strangely sentimental moment in this reunion of mass murderers.

> *Tex returned to C. A. resolutely*
> *Did he miss the girls, absolutely*
> *They'd blow kisses and wave*
> *To salute their old fave*
> *Tex Watson appeared such a cutie*

Watson then takes a seat in the gallery where he becomes temporarily indistinguishable amongst the crowd. The jury comes back in and DeCarlo takes the stand. Fitzgerald begins his questioning of DeCarlo reiterating that he does know Tex Watson from his stint at Spahn Ranch. Next Fitzgerald asks, "Do you recognize Mr. Watson in this courtroom?"[1] DeCarlo responds in the affirmative and Fitzgerald requests that he point Watson out in the crowd. Upon doing so, Fitzgerald requests that Judge Older ask Watson to stand.

If you could put yourself in the jury box right now you could imagine how this moment would jar you to attention. These twelve people have been listening to testimony in this case for three months now, much of which has to do with mass murders committed by this Tex Watson. This is a man who they have never seen before and are about to see for the very first time. As Watson rises, the collective jury understandably leans forward to take in the sight.

The impact of the moment is certainly not what Fitzgerald has been hoping for, as all the other defense attorneys have feared. As the jury takes in the sight of the tall lanky Watson, hair cut short and in his nicely dressed attire, he just doesn't present as the type of person who could manipulate the murders of multiple people. While Watson's complete absence might have left a shadow of a doubt, his actual appearance does more to diminish than enhance the sense of danger the jury might have connected to him.

JUAN FLYNN ~ On September 27, Juan Flynn is called to the witness stand by Bugliosi. This is the first time we've mentioned Flynn so allow us to provide some background. He is one of a handful of people in our story who becomes tangentially involved in the Manson Family only because he works at Spahn Ranch.

He is a 6' 5" cowboy, of Panamanian descent, and a bit of a character. When asked what his job is at the ranch, Flynn responds "manure shoveler."[2] On a more aromatic note, the tall rugged Flynn is also an aspiring actor having landed minor roles in multiple Western movies.

His relationship with Manson certainly seems situated toward the bizarre. Because of Flynn's size, strength, and rugged nature, Charlie makes multiple maneuvers to lure Flynn into becoming a member of the Family. But as is often the case with Panamanian cowboys, they tend to trend toward the stubborn end. Flynn doesn't mind being immersed in the Manson menagerie, but he has no desire to earn the merit badge for official Manson Scout membership. The sash would've looked funny on him anyway.

Upon entering the witness box, Flynn's demonstrates a distinctly different demeanor from anyone who has previously taken the stand. He's the only witness who actually seems to be having fun up there. In assessing previous witnesses, while some seemed intimidated by Manson, and others seemed able to ignore him, only Flynn seems to enjoy the confrontation. When Manson initiates his go-to strategy of the stare down, Flynn gleefully glares right back at him. Let the games begin!

In his testimony Flynn conveys that on one occasion during the second week of August 1969, he has just made a sandwich in the kitchen at Spahn and is sitting down to eat lunch with a handful of Family members in the room. Charlie walks in and makes a gesture swiping his right hand across his chest up to his left shoulder. This appears, to Flynn, to be the Family sign for everybody to leave the room, because within a few seconds Flynn and Manson are alone.

In an apparent last ditch effort to convince Flynn to try out for the team, Charlie gets in Flynn's face and says, "You're either with me or against me." Unintimidated, Flynn takes another bite of his sandwich. At this point, Manson grabs Flynn by the hair, pulls his head back, and holds a knife to his throat before threatening, "You son of a bitch, don't you know I'm the one doing all of these killings?"[3]

In terms of the transcript of the trial, this is certainly a breakthrough moment. For the first time a witness has essentially testified that Manson has confessed to the murders. Allow us to qualify this comment from the perspective that when Flynn hears Manson acknowledge the killings, he does not know what "killings" Manson is referring to, nor did the Panamanian cowboy particularly care.

Even with Manson holding a knife to his throat, Flynn feels sure that Charlie won't have the balls to go through with it. Not with half a sandwich on the plate, Charlie always hated to waste food.

Contributing to the cowboy's calmness is that, as Flynn testifies, "I thought Charlie was bullshitting. Who in his right mind is going to kill somebody and boast about it?"[4] While basically supporting Flynn's assessment of the situation, we're going to call him on one point.

One irony of the Manson trial that occurred to us as we wrote this book is that, if this is even possible, Manson's attorney Irving Kanarek becomes nearly as despicable as Manson by the end of the trial. When Juan Flynn makes the statement essentially conveying the fact that

Manson has admitted the murders to him, Kanarek is convinced of the need to disqualify Flynn's testimony.

Kanarek begins a line of questioning suggesting the fact that Flynn has recently fabricated the story about Manson's threat, pointing out that Flynn never mentioned the incident in his previous police interview with LAPD Detective Sartuchi. Continuing to challenge Flynn, Kanarek queries, "You were holding that back, is that it, Mr. Flynn to spring on us in this courtroom, is that right?"

Flynn answers, "No, I told the officers about this before, you see."

Choosing to assume Flynn's answer is a lie, Kanarek pushes on saying, "You mean, Mr. Flynn, that you made it up for the purposes of this courtroom, is that correct, Mr. Flynn?"[5]

Flynn's attempt to clarify this point shocks Bugliosi. Flynn says that at one previous interview in December, with the California Highway Patrol (CHP or *CHiPs* if you're old enough to remember the 1977-83 TV crime drama), he had shared the information about Manson's comment.

At the very next break in the proceedings, Bugliosi's reaction to this shocker is immediately questioning Flynn about the CHP interview. This could be huge! If this can be corroborated, it means that for the past nine months, the police have already possessed a recording about a Manson confession which nobody has documented. In such a high-profile case, this seems too bizarre to be true.

But alas, having come to know the LAPD as we have in this book, that is a bit of a bizarrerie that may be more predictable than unexpected. Does the LAPD have the confession tape? Of course they do. Here's the scoop.

Flynn does not remember the name of the police officer who interviewed him, but Bugliosi is hell-bent on figuring out who it was. This mystery ends up unraveling much more quickly and beneficially than one might have suspected. Just one phone call leads to the identification of the CHP officer who had interviewed Flynn at Death Valley as being Dave Stueber.

Upon making contact with Stueber, the officer checks his records and confirms that he had interviewed Flynn, along with three other men who had a presence on Barker Ranch. The interviews took place on December 19; all told they lasted nine hours, and he had taped the entire session. Bugliosi then asks Stueber if he can bring the tape to Los Angeles and testify at the trial. Stueber replies in the affirmative.

Next the news moves from shocking to absolutely mind-blowing. In reviewing his notes, Stueber passes on the additional information that he had already made a copy of the tape which had been sent to LAPD on December 29, 1969. So as of that date, LAPD had in its possession a tape in which Manson implicates himself in the Tate-LaBianca murders. The operative question becomes, what the hell happened to it?

Bugliosi is able to identify the LAPD officer who signed for the tapes, confirming their receipt. That officer admits he never played them, remembers giving the tapes to someone else, but cannot remember who that someone was. The tapes have definitely never been booked into evidence, and probably never even been played, just one more truly unbelievable example of the shoddy police work which characterizes this investigation.

CHARLIE'S LEAP ~ The day of October 5 proves to be an interesting one in the trial. As LASO Detective Paul Whiteley has just finished his testimony, Manson has a question for Judge Older, who is now said to be carrying a gun under his robe, just in case. He wants to know if he can question the witness, initiating yet another ugly exchange between Manson and Older, but this one elevates "ugly" to new heights.

What happens next probably qualifies as the single most memorable moment in the trial. It is also the most terrifying. With the spring of a caged animal escaping its confines, Manson leaps over the defense table and vaults himself a distance of literally ten feet, landing just a few feet in front of Judge Older's bench. Charlie has a sharpened pencil in his right hand.

Fortunately for everyone in the courtroom except Manson, the impact of the ten-foot leap causes him to drop to one knee. The brief time it takes him to recover proves just enough to allow bailiffs to prevent his progress toward the judge. As Manson is pinned to the floor, subdued and handcuffed, the girls provide a soundtrack to the saga rising and beginning a chant in Latin. What a show![6]

After jumping the table Chuck groped
Toward the judge where his balance said, "Nope"
Had Manson not slipped
The Judge was equipped,
But <u>not</u> using the gun was his hope

Manson has a parting gift for Judge Older. On his way out of the room Manson screams back, "In the name of Christian justice, someone should cut your head off."[7] Manson continues to fight tooth and nail all the way to his cell where it ultimately takes four bailiffs to secure him into the lock up.

Between the ladies, the leaping and the Latin the jury and courtroom spectators may have been uncertain as to whether they were watching a trial or a three-ring circus. Send in the clowns!

CHAPTER 20:
ENDING THE TESTIMONY
AS WELL AS THE HUGHES SAGA
(NOVEMBER 16, 1970-JANUARY 15, 1971)

TESTIMONY ENDS ~ Next, prepare yourself for some high drama in the courtroom. On November 16, the prosecution rests its case. Throughout the courthouse, rumors had been circulating that Manson has managed to mastermind some kind of a bombshell defense. However, rumors of that defense are devoid of details leaving all to open speculation. Three days later, after arguing standard dismissal motions, the defense stuns the court by resting its case, without calling a single witness.

This action by the defense shocks the entire courtroom, especially the defendants. The defense has become aware that it is their clients' goal to take the stand, supposedly in their own defense, and then falsely claim that they had planned and committed the murders with no knowledge of, or participation by, Charles Manson.

Knowing this can only result in a legal confirmation of their guilt, the defense team concludes that it is in the best interest of their clients not to call any witnesses at all. Rather, they will pin their hopes upon the possibility that the prosecution has not proven the defendants' guilt beyond the shadow of a doubt. Susan Atkins, Patricia Krenwinkel, and Leslie Van Houten all shout their disapproval and demand their right to testify.

When Judge Older speaks to the women's lawyers in chambers, the story behind "Charlie's Bombshell" is fully shared. Charlie's Angels are going to send him to Heaven and set him free by having all three of them take the stand with a strategy of united confession. They will all testify that they had planned and committed the murders themselves, and

Manson had no involvement whatsoever. Basically, they are so committed to Charlie that they are willing to take the fall for him.

Van Houten's lawyer Ronald Hughes specifically states, "I refuse to take part in any proceeding where I am forced to push a client out the window."[1] The lawyers justify their refusal to call witnesses because they are fully aware of the fact that their clients are being manipulated by Manson. The fuse has been snuffed out on Charlie's bombshell, perhaps.

In his chambers, with all five attorneys, Judge Older finds himself facing a question with a delicate balance. Two legal doctrines find themselves at odds in this situation. On one hand the girls have the right to testify, and on the other hand they also have the right to effective counsel. Oddly in this particular scenario, those two rights cancel each other out.

So what is the judge to do? Judge Older makes the determination that not only will the girls be allowed to testify, Manson will be also. When asked if he'd like to speak Charlie passes, at least for the moment. At this point Susan Atkins is sworn in and takes the stand. In the next move in this chess game, her lawyer Daye Shinn refuses to question her. So it's everybody back to the judge's chambers again, where Older makes it clear he will not allow the defense to sabotage the case.

Charles Manson turns the tide with a surprise announcement for everyone the following morning. He has decided that he does want to testify. Invoking a California law that specifies juries cannot hear testimony of one defendant implicating the guilt of a co-defendant, Judge Older has the jury removed from the courtroom. After being sworn in, Manson chooses the option of making a statement rather than being questioned by his attorney.

Manson's statement goes on for over an hour. During this time he rambles through various components of his philosophy. His speech features various styles of delivery almost as if he is playing multiple characters in a one-man show. Just to convey a feel for Manson's statement, we have excerpted a handful of passages that stood out to us for one reason or another.

"You made your children what they are. These children that come at you with knives, they are your children. You taught them. I didn't teach them. I just tried to help them stand up. Most of the people at the ranch that you call 'the Family' were just people that you did not want, people that were alongside the road, that their parents had kicked out, that did not want to go to juvenile hall. So I did the best I could and I took them up and I told them this, that in love there is no wrong."

"I told them that anything they do for their brothers and sisters is good if they do it with a good thought. I was working at cleaning up my house, something that Nixon should have been doing. He should have been on the side of the road, picking up his children, but he wasn't. He was in the White House sending them off to war. I know that in your hearts and souls you are as much responsible for the Vietnam War as I am for killing these people."

"I can't judge any of you. I have no malice against you and no ribbons for you. But I think that it's high time that you all start looking at yourselves. The music is telling the kids to rise up against the establishment. Why blame it on me? I didn't write the music. I have killed no one and I have ordered no one to be killed. I may have implied on several different occasions, to several different people, that I may have been Jesus Christ, but I haven't decided yet what I am or who I am." After finishing his testimony, Charlie passes by the defense table and tells the girls, 'You don't have to testify now.'"[2]

On November 20, after the defense logs in all of its evidence, Judge Older issues a ten-day recess which is the standard time allowed for jury instructions and arguments to be prepared by both legal teams. Leslie Van Houten's lawyer Ronald Hughes feels that, of all the defendants' attorneys, he has the greatest reason for optimism. Van Houten had not been present at the Tate murders and while she had stabbed, Rosemary LaBianca, the suggestion had been made that the victim was already dead by the time Van Houten had become a participant.

Gathering the pertinent papers, Ronald Hughes leaves to spend the weekend at his favorite campsite, 130 miles away at Sespe Hot Springs. On November 30, when the court resumes, Hughes is absent. None of the other defense attorneys has any knowledge of his whereabouts. He will never be seen alive again.

In the immediate aftermath of Hughes' disappearance, multiple theories are floated. There had been flooding in the Sespe Hot Springs area and the terrain there was rugged. Hughes (remember, he was the "hippie" lawyer) had departed on Friday, riding up to the mountains in a Volkswagen, accompanied by a teenage hippie couple with whom he was friends. His friends however changed their minds and decided to go back to L.A. that night. Discovering that their Volkswagen was mired in the mud, they nonetheless decided to hitchhike home.

These somewhat bizarre details might seem to put the teenage hippie couple at the top of the suspect list. But Hughes was seen on Saturday morning by three boys who happened to cross his path at his campsite. A brief conversation was shared and the boys reported that at the time, Hughes did not seem ill or injured and his mood was upbeat. He was also safe, at a relatively high location away from the flooding. The hippies are off the hook. And the three boys subsequently pass polygraph tests, also clearing them.

One line of conjecture suggests the possibility that Hughes, overwhelmed by the trial, had taken off to avoid the final argument phase. Upon investigation of his home, some unusual findings lend this conjecture some credence. Hughes was living in the garage of a friend, sleeping on a mattress on the concrete floor. His one room bachelor pad is strewn with so much debris one reporter wrote, "I wouldn't let my dog sleep there."[3] Hanging neatly on the wall is his framed bar certificate.

Another theory is that, in a final ill-conceived attempt to salvage a failing defense, he had skipped town in order to throw a monkey wrench into the trial's proceedings. The fact that Hughes never resurfaces does indeed rock the judicial boat. When Judge Older, on December 2, decides that a replacement attorney must be appointed, it imposes a two-week delay in the trial to allow for the new lawyer, Maxwell Keith, to review the 18,000 pages of trial transcripts which had been generated by that point.

Returning to the campsite at Sespe Hot Springs, inclement weather delays a helicopter search for two days. When the choppers go airborne, they find nothing. Accessing the area on foot, investigators find the abandoned Volkswagen but no sign of Hughes. In the abandoned

Volkswagen some of the court transcripts are found, but not all the papers Hughes is known to have brought with him are still there. Conspicuously absent... a secret psychiatric report on Leslie Van Houten.

Continuing in our writing strategy to complete subplots in their entirety rather than become slaves of chronological order, we are now going to fast forward to the conclusion of the Hughes story. His body is not found until April. The body has deteriorated to the point where the cause of death cannot be determined. Various Family members have already taken claim for the death prior to the discovery of the body. No one is ever charged.

Protecting Van Houten, Ron Hughes blocks
Her confessing on the court soap box
As the verdict went down
His dead body was found
Face down and wedged under two big rocks

At this point, having completed the subplot of Ronald Hughes' death, allow us to share a quick timeline to connect the dots between the November 30 court continuance when Hughes' absence was first noted, and the December 21 date when the trial resumes.

DECEMBER 6: Paul Fitzgerald ominously shares with reporters his belief that, "He may well be dead - it seems probably at this point."[4]

DECEMBER 7: The Los Angeles Sheriff's Office issues an all-points bulletin, which of course is something you do when you have no other leads.

DECEMBER 8: Judge Older goes to the Ambassador Hotel and delivers the ultimate holiday buzzkill to the jury. He informs them of the reason for the delay in their return to the courtroom and also that said delay will result in them remaining sequestered throughout the entire holiday season. Jingle all the way!

While pondering deliberation
The jury survives sequestration
But things don't go well then
The judge has to tell them
You will have no Christmas vacation

DECEMBER 12: The search for Ronald Hughes is suspended.

DECEMBER 15: Attorney Fitzgerald (for Krenwinkel) confides to Shinn (for Atkins) that he suspects, their colleague Hughes (for Van Houten) may have been targeted by the Family because he spearheaded the initiative that the defense would rest immediately and bring no witnesses to the stand.

DECEMBER 18: In response to the acid overdose murder attempt of Barbara Hoyt, a grand jury indicts Squeaky Fromme, Ruth Ann Moorehouse, Steve Grogan (aka Clem), Catherine Share (aka Gypsy) and Dennis Rice for conspiracy to prevent and dissuade a witness from attending a trial. In a quirkily related side note we will share the fact that there is no such thing as a fatal overdose of LSD. The drug could possibly lead someone into a foolhardy act that could result in death, (like jumping off a building,) but the drug itself does not cause death.

DECEMBER 21: Court reconvenes.

On December 21, court reconvenes with a substitution being inserted into the defense's new starting lineup. If this trial were a sports competition, the PA announcer might have said, "Entering the action for the defense is new attorney Maxwell Keith, replacing the missing Ronald Hughes." Not the way the game should be played.

Keith begins the reconvened session with what can be considered a calculated ploy. He motions Judge Older that, "While I now feel familiar with the evidence from having read the transcripts, having not been present for the testimony of the witnesses, nor having seen their demeanor during said testimony, I am not confident that I can responsibly represent Leslie Van Houten."[5]

Recognizing this obvious ploy, Judge Older denies the motion and rules that the show must go on. Our use of the cliché "the show must go on" was inadvertent as we originally wrote this. But in retrospect, as we reread our composition, the phrase becomes particularly apropos. This entire trial has been a show in one sense or another, and one that would be truly in the running for the show of the century. We're going to name our show the *Celebratory Circus of Surreal Sensationalism*. Tickets are available at the box office.

As has become a somewhat expected component of the show, there is an opening act, featuring Maniac Manson and Charlie's Angels, which has been contrived to assure their removal from the judicial proceedings on a somewhat regular basis. Here's what happens on this particular day. In addition to getting them kicked out of the courtroom, this act serves as a commentary serving to reflect the Family's loss of power.

Wavering wildly and wickedly from what his weapon wielding ways once were, Charlie looks for the most deadly projectile available in his immediate surroundings. Deciding upon his weapon of choice, Charlie grabs a paper clip and throws it at Judge Older. The girls earn their free pass out of the room by chanting an accusation that the judge was responsible for doing away with Hughes.

Once these games are concluded, it becomes time for Bugliosi to make his closing statement to the jury. In real time, this thing drags on for three days. We can already hear you thanking us for making it the short version which we will share with you here. Bugliosi basically replays and summarizes the entire trial on a witness-by-witness basis. You've already read the important parts of everything he says.

In summarizing what has taken place over the past six months, Bugliosi feels he has, beyond all reasonable doubt, established Manson's overriding motive, his control over the Family, and his involvement with the crimes. In regard to Atkins, Krenwinkel and Van Houten, he has established their subservient service to Manson and how this led to their participation in the crimes.

All of the attorneys have the opportunity to offer a final summary to the jury. This having taken place, Judge Older addresses the jury and sends them out to begin deliberations. The date is January 15, 1971; it is seven months, to the day, from when this trial commenced.

CHAPTER 21:
YOUR HONOR, WE HAVE A VERDICT
(JANUARY 16-MARCH 25, 1971)

DELIBERATIONS BEGIN ~ The deliberations start on that Friday and will end up running ten days. During this period there are only two specific requests made of Judge Older. The jury asks to be able to play the Beatles' *White Album* and requests to visit the Tate and LaBianca residences. Older honors their Beatles request but denies the crime scene visitations feeling they might open a Pandora's box tantamount to retrying the case.

> *The jury asks judge to procure*
> *The White Album and crime scene tour*
> *Though you want to go*
> *The field trip's a "No"*
> *But I'll give you the album for sure*

On the afternoon of January 25, 1971, the jury informs Judge Older that they have reached a verdict. Imagine the drama in the courtroom. Right now allow us to take you there and share with you how it goes down live at the reading of the verdict.

JUDGE: All jurors and alternates are present. All counsel but Mr. Hughes are present. The defendants are present. Mr. Tubick, has the jury reached a verdict?
TUBICK: Yes, Your Honor, we have.
JUDGE: Will you hand the verdict forms to the bailiff.

(After receiving the forms from the bailiff Judge Older peruses them carefully. Manson and the girls are silent.)

JUDGE: The clerk will read the verdicts.

CLERK: In the Superior Court of the State of California, in and for the County of Los Angeles, the People of the State of California vs. Charles Manson, Patricia Krenwinkel, Susan Atkins, and Leslie Van Houten. We, the jury in the above-entitled action, find the defendant Charles Manson, guilty of the crime of murder.[1]

There are 27 verdicts to be read altogether, so it takes some time, but every verdict comes back guilty. The defendants all sit silently, displaying no emotion.

PENALTY PHASE ~ Once the verdicts are all rendered, the process moves on to the penalty phase of the trial. Given the circumstances of the charges in this case, there isn't a lot of ways this one can go. The only two options at the disposal of the jury are the death penalty, or life in prison.

But there is still some tension involved with this piece of the process. While Manson seems a lock for the death penalty, might the girls get off with life sentences, their culpability having been mitigated by the fact that they were so controlled by Manson? And even amongst the three girls there clearly exists two tiers of guilt.

While Susan Atkins and Patricia Krenwinkel had actively participated in both nights of the killing spree, Leslie Van Houten had only been involved with the LaBiancas. Furthermore, it could be argued that Rosemary LaBianca might have already been dead when Van Houten stabbed her.

Granted, plunging a knife into the dead body of a murder victim multiple times is certainly not an act which would garner a Girl Scout merit badge, but does that, in and of itself, merit a death penalty? Viewing the crimes through this prism certainly allows for the possibility of a mixed decision on the girls with Atkins and Krenwinkel getting the death sentence while Van Houten receives life in prison.

The penalty phase of the trial is most unique because of the fact that it brings into the courtroom many of the Manson Family members who have essentially been barred throughout the proceedings. Flashing back to much earlier in the book, we should probably refresh your memory as to how and why this funky Family freak show had effectively been banned from the trial.

Let's go to a hypothetical *Jeopardy!* TV show, including a category of "Courtroom Procedures". If Alec Trebek states that the clue is, "Put them on the list of potential witnesses who could be called upon to testify, even though there's no chance whatsoever you would actually call them as witnesses", the question would be, "If you're a legal team, how do you keep people out of the courtroom who you'd rather not have there?"

Bottom line, the defense team absolutely does not want an assembly of cultish hippies dominating the courtroom audience who would, by association alone, cast aspersions upon their clients. So just in case you've missed the gist of our *Jeopardy!* question above, and also to embellish upon the explanation a bit, here's the story behind this legal strategy. Any persons who are put on the list of prospective witnesses by lawyers in a trial, are forbidden to attend any other portions of said trial to assure they are not influenced by the testimony of other witnesses.

In preparing for the trial, the defense team lists every known Manson Family member as a potential witness, not because there was ever any actual intent to call upon them to testify, but only because it proves to be a means of proficiently precluding their presence at the proceedings.

So going back to the concept we introduced four paragraphs ago, this penalty phase of the trial adds a new level of interest because we get to hear directly from Family members who heretofore have been only tangentially involved, reduced to the rank of street soldiers prowling in the proximity of the courthouse.

With the conclusion of the guilt phase of the trial, the banning of potential witnesses is also concluded. This allows for Manson's Family members to be called in by defense attorneys to testify in regard to their feelings about whether or not the defendants should get the death penalty.

Earlier in the trial, Judge Older had encouraged the defense attorneys to intervene positively in situations where their clients' behavior was inappropriate. Patricia Krenwinkel's attorney, Paul Fitzgerald, while acknowledging the wisdom of the judge's intentions, adds the reality that "there is a minimum of client control in this case."[2] So brace yourself. When there are just four Family members present, the calamities of catastrophic courtroom chaos created were cacophonous. Image what might happen when the entire Family gets to filter through the courtroom.

The point in this piece of the court process is that parties sympathetic to the convicted defendants are allowed to express to the jury the reasons why they feel the defendants might be worthy of the lesser of the two possible sentences. The only part of this process that seems to potentially portend positively for the defendants is a poignant parental participation piece.

The defense strategy of immediately pulling in the parents to provide any testimony that might serve to spin a sympathetic sway in salvaging the life of their child manages to strike a few chords. In reading the transcript, our take on this is that it was a mistake on the part of the attorneys to lead with the parents.

Please allow us to explain our perceived mistake in the defense strategy and we'll proceed in appropriately militaristic Manson terms. In a bevy of military clichés, we hope won't leave you "gun-shy;" we'll "fire off the shot" that the defense prematurely "brought out the heavy artillery". They "jumped the gun" and "shot their wad" much too early. Bottom line... the defense should have sent the fanatical Family members in to take the stand first and saved the more respectable and sympathetic parents for the grand finale.

After the testimony by the parents, various Family members are called to the stand and afforded the opportunity to spin whatever positive thoughts they can about the defendants. As one might expect, this whole process is a disjointed disarray of Manson-inspired musings. It's difficult to discern any thread of a cohesive strategy as the Family forays to the witness stand but, truth be told, with such an undisciplined group, any organized strategy would have been difficult to pursue.

In reverting to our oft stated approach of striking the best balance between entertaining you and informing you, we are hereby condensing hundreds of transcript pages into a few paragraphs. As we trudged through those aforementioned pages the thread which most caught our interest was that of Charlie's Family attributing to him Christ-like powers.

If during the penalty phase of the trial Charlie's Angels had any chance of delaying his gas chamber-induced entrance to Heaven, that purpose would have been best served by portraying him as just one of the guys on the Family team as opposed to a Christ-like savior. It would have been better off for Manson if the Family did not seem so irrationally devoted to him.

Signing on to sing Charlie's praises
The Angels' storyline these days is
If they'd just kept their mouths shut
They might have saved his butt
His chances just went up in blazes

That being said, please allow us to specify some highlights of the 2000 pages of testimony we covered from this phase of the trial. Periodically, through the course of this book, references have been made to Manson being referred to, and viewed as, a Jesus Christ figure. When given the opportunity to testify during the sentencing phase of not only Charles Manson, but also the girls, here are a couple passages shared by some members of the Family.

Brenda McCann says, "Charlie would sit down and all the animals would gather around him. Mountain goats, donkeys and coyotes and things. Even snakes, one time he reached down and petted a rattlesnake."[4] Everybody needs a pet, right?

Sandra Good says, "I believe his voice could shatter this building if he so desired. Once he yelled and a window broke. One time Charlie found a dead bird in the desert, breathed upon it, and brought it back to life."[5] Not sure where Penn and Teller were when this one took place, but we remain skeptical.

And while Charlie's Angels are attempting to come to his aid, how ironic is it that Mother Nature manages to step in and provide him with an unneeded assist. At 6:01 am on February 9, 1970, an earthquake registering 6.5 on the Richter scale rocks L.A. claiming 65 lives. At the Ambassador Hotel, where the jury is staying, the earthquake breaks pipes causing them to be unexpectedly showered by water from the sprinkler system.

A few hours later, when everyone involved with the trial is recovering from the shock and arriving at the L.A. courthouse, the Family members circling the grounds resolve the mystery for them. Everyone arriving is assured that Charlie has caused the earthquake. If you haven't retrieved your Bible and recently read Revelation, Chapter 9, it is time to do so.

> *On an evening that's highly romancin'*
> *The girls out at Spahn Ranch are dancin'*
> *The quake hits L.A.*
> *All bow down and pray*
> *To our savior whose name's Charles Manson*

Probably appropriately, Manson's devout disciples cannot resist using their testimony time downloading their devotion. While it might have been gratifying to the disciples at the time, it actually serves to compromise Charlie's cause. As stated, Manson would have been better off if his disciples' testimony had served to humanize him rather than deitize him. The accolades only serve to confirm the concept that the disciples are all acting at the behest of their spiritual leader.

After all the testimony has been given in the penalty phase, each of the defense attorneys gets one final opportunity to plea their client's case to the jury. Irving Kanarek leads off with his plea on behalf of Charles Manson. This is one of those places in the book where we'll keep it short and sweet. Kanarek speaks for over a day, using the bulk of that time to quote Bible verses from the New Testament.

As has characterized Kanarek throughout the trial, he has a propensity for the preposterous. We've made that point before. We'll give you one last sampling here. At one point in his statement Kanarek says, "Now, this being the Easter season, there is an analogy here between Mr. Manson; this may sound at first blush to be ridiculous, and we are not suggesting that Mr. Manson is the deity, or Christ-like, or anything like that; but how can we know?"[6] Hmmm... we're thinking a more effective approach might have been to proffer the theory that Charles Manson was really the Easter Bunny.

Speaking on behalf of Susan Atkins, Daye Shinn focuses on Vincent Bugliosi's convincing Atkins to tell her story to the grand jury in the earliest phases of the trial. Shinn states that, "Ms. Atkins was drowning, without friends, and she sees Mr. Bugliosi with an oar. She says, 'Oh here comes help now.' Ms. Atkins reached out for that oar and what do you think Mr. Bugliosi did? He hit her over the head with the oar."[7] Nautical imagery notwithstanding, this seems to us like a pretty thin line of reasoning to justify why Susan Atkins should not have to walk the plank.

Next Maxwell Keith speaks on behalf of Leslie Van Houten. Rather than attacking Bugliosi, Keith adopts an alternate strategy of looking for points where he agrees with the prosecuting attorney before making his final pitch for Van Houten's life. Regarding Bugliosi, Keith says, "I accept his exposition to you that Mr. Manson dominated these girls and ordered the homicides. I accept his telling you that you shouldn't hold the Hinman murder against Leslie. I accept his argument that the testimony of the other girls in this case shows that Mr. Manson's domination and influence still persists and is all-pervasive."

"Mr. Manson is insane and Leslie Van Houten has been infected with his madness. Give Leslie the chance for redemption to which she is entitled. Remember, Linda Kasabian cut the umbilical cord, in Mr. Bugliosi's words, that tied her to Manson and his Family. Give Leslie the chance to do the same. Give her life."[8]

On behalf of Patricia Krenwinkel, Paul Fitzgerald takes yet another strategy. He attempts to elicit pity by providing a detailed and graphic description of the process of death in the gas chamber. Bugliosi initially objects on the basis that this is an improper argument, but after a discussion at the bench, Fitzgerald is allowed to proceed. Having been instructed by Judge Older, the jury leaves for their final deliberation at 5:25 pm on Friday, March 26, 1971.

CHAPTER 22:
DEATH BE NOT PROUD
(MARCH 29-OCTOBER 21, 1971)

On the following Monday, they will be back in the courtroom with verdicts. Knowing this will be their final opportunity to collectively create courtroom chaos, the Manson team makes the most of it. Upon making their entry, it is impossible to miss the fact that the girls have a sporty new look. Mimicking Charlie, all three have shaved their heads.

Before any of the verdicts have been read, Manson launches into his final tirade of the trial. "I don't see how you can get by with this without letting me put on some kind of defense," Charlie screams. "You people have no authority over me."[1] As Manson continues his rant, Older has him removed from the courtroom for the final time.

Following that, the clerk reads the first verdict saying, "We, the jury in the above-entitled action, having found the defendant Charles Manson guilty of murder in the first degree as charged in count one of the indictment, do now fix the penalty as death."[2] This prompts a clearly choreographed 1-2-3 response on the part of the girls.

Patricia Krenwinkel says, "You have just judged yourselves."[3] Susan Atkins follows with, "Better lock your doors and watch your own kids."[4] And Leslie Van Houten concludes with, "Your whole system is a game, you blind stupid people. Your children will turn against you."[5] At this point Judge Older has the girls removed. It would be through the audio feed in their lockup that Patricia, Susan and Leslie would hear that they have also been sentenced to death.

Meanwhile, back in the courtroom, there is a collectively celebratory sigh of relief shared by the jurors. After 225 days of sequestration they are finally free! At that point in time, in the annals of American crime history, no jury had ever been sequestered longer. Finally, able to engage with them on a friendly personal level, Judge Older shakes hands with each juror and lauds them with praise. "If it were within the power of a judge to award a medal of honor to jurors," he says, "believe me, I would bestow an award on each of you for service above and beyond the call of duty."[6]

Next, how about this little cherry of a coincidence to put on top? As we shared with you earlier, on March 29, the very same day the jury recommends death sentences, the body of Leslie Van Houten's attorney Ronald Hughes is discovered in Ventura County a few miles from where his campsite had been. Because of the decomposition of the body, the cause of death cannot be determined. The body is found wedged between two boulders, lying face down.

There is one final step to be taken in the legal process. After the penalty phase, when the jury returns the verdict voicing its choice regarding the fate of the defendants, there still remains a final court appearance where the judge makes the sentence official. A judge does have the power to reverse the jury's verdict if that verdict is felt to be inappropriate. The sentencing date is set for April 19, 1971.

All four defendants have the right to speak. Only Manson does. Surprisingly, it's not the Mansonian tirade you might expect. Trembling, looking noticeably tired and near tears, Charlie just says, "I accept this court as my father. I have always done my best in life to uphold the laws of my father, and I accept my father's judgment."[7]

Judge Older responds by saying, "After nine and a half months of trial, all of the superlatives have been used, all of the hyperbole has been indulged in, and all that remains are the bare, stark facts of seven senseless murders, seven people whose lives were snuffed out by total strangers. I have carefully looked, in considering this action, for mitigating circumstances, and I have been unable to find any. It is my considered judgment that not only is the death penalty appropriate, but it is almost compelled by the circumstances. I must agree with the prosecutor that if this is not a proper case for the death penalty, what would be?"[8]

The defendants sat there all aghast
That gas chamber's not such a blast
But media knew
The fans would come through
If the killings could be simulcast

Judge Older completes the judicial process by confirming the death penalty sentence upon all four defendants. So at this point we will address an obvious question which has to be flashing in the minds of most everybody reading this book that knows they have recollections of Manson interviews, later in his life. What changes?

It all changes as a result of a 1972 California Supreme Court trial. In that year, the case of the California Supreme Court's "People vs. Anderson" decision results in the invalidation of all death sentences imposed in California prior to 1972.[9] Not that this court decision is directly related to the Manson trial, but it has obvious manifestations.

As our story winds down, allow us to share with you this interesting side story. All California death row prisoners were housed in separate facilities from other inmates, and for men there were multiple such facilities. Because the number of women on death row was comparatively much smaller, every death row California female was imprisoned in the same facility.

As fate would have it, Susan Atkins, Patricia Krenwinkel and Leslie Van Houten all served their death row time within speaking distance of each other. For the first year of their mutual incarceration they had no option but to share thoughts about their impending deaths.

Not that they had the ability to throw a big party, but imagine the mood swing when on February 18, 1972, the State of California decides that they would all live out their full lives, albeit behind bars. Susan Atkins remembered her first words upon hearing that proclamation as being, "Thank God. I want to thank you for letting me live, and all the others too."[10] She would go on to become a born-again Christian.

Subsequently, rather than the story and its direct participants having all been put to death by the end of the decade, Manson along with his disciples would survive until old age enabling them to write books, conduct interviews, and continue to keep the story alive to a much greater degree than would have been possible if they all had been executed.

We've added a Bonus Chapter 2 (available only in the print version of this book) which we call "Character Backstories." This originally started in a vein of "Where are they now?" but with the 50th anniversary of the crimes approaching obviously the answer for the majority of people involved would be "buried in the ground". That being said, there were a handful of participants still alive and kicking when we wrote this book in 2019. One, Bobby Beausoleil, was even conducting a successful business, from behind bars, marketing his music and artwork.

TEX WATSON ~ We need an end-story for the Tex Watson thread of this since he is not involved in the trial. Watson leaves the Spahn Ranch on October 2, 1969, and returns to his native Texas. He is arrested there on November 30, 1969, but manages to avoid extradition for nine months, preventing his inclusion in the first trial. As we discussed earlier in the book, his return to California does not occur until close to the end of the first trial in late 1970.

Subsequently, we want to include these few paragraphs on the Tex topic to share how his story plays out. His trial begins in August 1971, and lasts a relatively short period of time. He is found guilty on seven counts of first degree murder and one count of conspiracy to commit murder on October 21, 1971. After returning these guilty verdicts, the jury takes just 2½ hours of deliberation on the punishment before returning a death sentence. As is the case with the earlier defendants, his death sentence is overturned by the 1972 decision of the California Supreme Court.

> *Returning upon extradition*
> *Tex does finally show some contrition*
> *But he'll be in jail*
> *Of course without fail*
> *To get out he'd need a magician*

CHAPTER 23:
SUMMING UP FAMILY MATTERS
(OCTOBER 22, 1971-NOVEMBER 19, 2017)

INTERVIEWS ~ After being imprisoned for life, Charles Manson does participate in some very interesting interviews. We watched these several times and developed some analyses and conclusions on his speaking strategies. Characterizing all of these is his consistent proclamation of innocence. Keep in mind that as he manipulates his narrative, he has working to his advantage the fact that he, personally, did not kill anyone. His basic shtick is to talk in circles in what we came to call "rehearsed rambling."

Another technique Manson employs in speaking is the occasional use of nonsense syllable gibberish. The sounds emanating from his mouth are not even close to being words. If one was to take him as a Christ figure, it's like he's speaking in tongues. Here's our take on this. In general, his pace of speech is always rapid. If, in his cyclical monologue, he temporarily draws a blank he will tread water by reverting to his nonsensical gibberish in order to keep his audience engaged while simultaneously giving himself time to think of where he wants to go next.

In proclaiming his innocence, obviously the challenge he faces is distancing himself from the orders he gave to his followers. Here is the typical approach he takes in that effort. He says things like, "I gave Tex and the girls a reality, and they chose what to do with that reality. What they did with that reality is on them not me. I never killed nobody." One note on the previous sentence... although we put it in quotation marks it is not a specific quote from a single source. It is, based upon all the interviews we watched, us taking Manson's standard spiel and putting it into our own words.

GERALDO RIVERA - In 1988, Geraldo Rivera interviewed Manson for a special he did called "Devil Worship: Exposing Satan's Underground." Watching the entire interview, including the excerpts not included in the special, is truly revealing. We honestly felt that Manson got the better of Rivera in the confrontation.

Manson consistently foils Rivera's attempts to get him to admit to anything. There are times during the interview when Rivera is clearly frustrated and angry. Manson however stays calm and awaits opportunities to go on the offensive. Here is one example of this.

Going into this interview, Rivera seems to have made it his personal goal to trip up Manson and extract from him some kind of admission or confession. At one point Manson makes the statement that he's in harmony with God. Clearly trying to derail him, Geraldo comes back with, "God or the Devil, Charlie?"

At this point Manson's eyes light up and he says, "Okay I'll play, there's no game I can't play."

Geraldo says, "You are the Devil, Charlie."

Manson responds, "Okay, I'll be the devil then," clearly conveying that he's on board with whatever little role-playing game Geraldo Is trying to orchestrate. At this stage of the game, the frustration visibly registers on Geraldo's face. His goal had been to lead Manson into some made-for-TV moment where the adept interviewer is able to lead his target into a well-coerced confession. Manson, however, manages to frustrate Geraldo by turning it all into a game.

CHARLIE ROSE - Manson's look in the Charlie Rose CBS interview is unique in that he has a long beard which is groomed into a fork. Very devilish. Here are a few highlights from that interview.

Rose asks Manson if he ever reads books, to which he responds, "My thoughts are more interesting than anything I could read."

About religion Manson says, "Spiritualism scares you people, because you've got this little stereotyped church that you're buying and selling, you're trying to put God in a building, but God is much bigger than that little church."

Knowing how infatuated he was with the Beatles, it was hard to tell if he was being facetious or not, but when asked about music Manson said, "I come from the heart of Bing Crosby, Frank Sinatra, and Tom Mix."

There was only one point during the interview when Rose seemed to have Manson back on his heels a bit. It was when Rose asked the following question. "Do you want to look back on the early part of your life, before the 60's and say, Boy something went wrong? Because, I got on this track and I was in and out of prison you know and I went to foster homes and then my mother would take me and then I would go see my grandmother and then go I'd go back and see my mother and then she would run away and somehow, did that shape you, did that make a difference?"

There was a long pregnant pause as Manson seemed to be searching for some agitated repartee to divert attention from topics he would rather not visit, as is his typical style. Charlie seems to pretty much come up empty on this one, ending the long pause by saying, "Well, see, that doesn't even compute in my world."

DIANE SAWYER ~ The interview we saw, that we found the most fascinating, was the one done in 1993 by Diane Sawyer for an ABC News "20/20" special, "Truth and Lies: The Family Manson." In the raw footage of this, the most intriguing part is a scene at the end where the camera is still rolling for a couple of minutes but Charlie doesn't realize it.

Manson's persona in the time after the interview is significantly different. When he knows he's being interviewed, it's almost like he assumes the role of a character in a play. He goes into that "rehearsed rambling" mode we described above.

In closing, Diane Sawyer clearly signals the end of the segment by saying, "We're done." At that point the crew begins to pack up equipment. The scene that follows is truly bizarre. Manson comes out of his "rehearsed rambling" mode and engages in the most shockingly normal conversation with Sawyer, which is captured by a single camera that remains recording.

INTERVIEW OVER ~ Actually the ambiance of the entire room takes on a rather startling air. The conversation takes place while Sawyer, and then various other members of the ABC news crew, cozy up with Manson one-by-one, to get their pictures taken. Manson tells the photographer that he would like copies of the pictures. The whole scene is one of joking and camaraderie.

We were so intrigued by this scene that we put together a transcript for you below. If you'd like to see it yourself allow us to help you with the following directions. There are a handful of Charles Manson/Diane Sawyer videos on YouTube. The one that contains the footage we describe above and below is the one that times in at 19:52.

By listening and re-listening to this audio multiple times, we have put together the following transcript for you. Keep in mind that, as we stated, the mood in general during this post-interview conversation is very casual, involving multiple speakers. There are a few parts where the speech is inaudible and there are a few lines that seem so insignificant we chose to omit them. We'll begin with Diane Sawyer's line to indicate the interview is over.

SAWYER: We're done.
             (There is some rustling and a pause while wires and mics are disconnected.)
MANSON: *(to Sawyer)* Have a good day.
             (Note: At one point during the interview the ABC crew had asked Manson if he needed anything and he asked if he could go to the bathroom.)
SAWYER: You'd think of all the questions I'd expect you to ask them *(her crew)* "Can I go to the bathroom?" is not the [first] one that would come to mind.
             (It is during this time that the ABC crew are, one-by-one, cozying up to Manson for pictures.)
MANSON: Hey, look here man, are you going to send me a copy of [these]?
PHOTOGRAPHER: Sure, the still pictures?
MANSON: Yeah, I been trying to get a still one for a long time, man.
PHOTOGRAPHER: I don't know, we gotta ask the prison.

MANSON: You don't have to ask the mailroom, they do things like that [for me].
                 (Charlie laughs.)

PHOTOGRAPHER: Charlie, they probably want to get their picture taken with you.
                 (Charlie leans in and smiles.)

MANSON: Let me look serious.
                 (Charlie shakes his head and assumes his perfected evil-eye glare.)

PHOTOGRAPHER: Get one with Diane.

MANSON: *(to Diane, showing he'd done his homework)* You're from Kentucky, huh?

SAWYER: Uh huh.

MANSON: What part?

SAWYER: I was born in the south, near Tennessee and grew up in Louisville.
                 (Note: The "CC Camps" Manson mentions next were part of FDR's New Deal and were a program designed to assist unemployed young men help their families during the Great Depression.)

MANSON: My Uncle Wormy died in Louisville trying to save the atmosphere. When the Tennessee Valley Authority came in, we started CC Camps back then. My grandfather started CC Camps before the Second World War, and then when the war came on, they forgot the CC Camps. It's just sad that there wasn't more of them.

SAWYER: You were born in Ohio, weren't you?

MANSON: My mother ran off from Ashland, Kentucky and went to Ohio.

PHOTOGRAPHER: *(speaking to Manson)* Diane says everybody wants a picture of you.

MANSON: Don't forget me on [copies of] those pictures.

PHOTOGRAPHER: Well, we'll ask the jail.
                 (There is an ongoing frenzy of picture requests)

PHOTOGRAPHER: Click, Click, Click. Everybody wants a picture of you, Charlie.
(Manson leans forward and once again, right on cue, assumes his evil-eye persona.)

MANSON: *(Interestingly well aware of his own persona.)* Everybody likes that evil character they created. You know, that guy with the eyes!
(Knowing he's delivered a killer closing line, no pun intended, Manson gets up to leave.)

PRISON GUARD: Charlie, you were real nice.

We thought that last line above was telling. Charles Manson had a unique ability to win people over with his charisma. Ironically, what he had done to that old prison guard who had the last line above, was basically the same thing he did to win over all the young kids he brought into his Family. Charlie was a chilling charmer.

On November 19, 2017, at the age of 83, Charles Manson died of a heart attack and complications from colon cancer. While he did not have access to the money, at the time of his death Manson's net worth was estimated at $400,000.[1] *Fortune* magazine reported on the "staggering" amount of Manson merchandise available for purchase, such as stickers, patches, and T-shirts — as well as the fact that Manson sold art online that he had created in prison. He did receive a small profit from some merchandise; according to a 1993 article from *The New York Times*, Manson received 10 cents for each $17 T-shirt sold featuring his likeness and the words "Charlie Don't Surf."[2]

Right now, Dennis Wilson is turning over in his grave.

BONUS CHAPTER 1:
THE BEATLES AND THE BIBLE

When Charles Manson first hears the Beatles, he is in prison on McNeil Island in Washington. He is so taken by the band that he breaks open his prison piggy bank, extracts whatever jailhouse favors he has stockpiled, and swaps them for guitar lessons from a fellow inmate who knows how to play. It is a fateful moment. Here are two predictions few would have made at the time. Between then and the end of the decade, man will have landed on the moon and Charles Manson will have recorded an album with the Beach Boys. Surf's Up!

Despite the connection with the Beach Boys, the musical influence that has far and away the most impact on Manson, as well as the world, will be the connection established between Manson and the Beatles. It will be their lyrics which will be used by Manson to develop one of the most criminally heinous and insane philosophies in the annals of crime history. Manson calls it "Helter Skelter" and we'll explain it below.

If you analyze the history of the Charles Manson Family and their connection to Beatles music, 1967 is the year of the cat, so to speak. During that year there are two significant releases. Charles Manson is released from jail and the Beatles release *The Magical Mystery Tour* album. Invoking the universal question of which came first, for the record (no pun intended), Manson is released in March and the album comes out in November.

Within weeks of his release, Manson is in San Francisco embracing and thriving in the Summer of Love. The Grateful Dead is first ascending to fame bringing to mind their catch phrase of "What a long strange trip it's been." The LSD reference can't be ignored. Manson is about to lead himself and his followers on one of the strangest three-year trips imaginable.

Manson recruits his first female followers and as everybody knows, if you are going to go on a genuine 1960's hippie trip, a bus is a must. So they buy one, tear out most of the seats, create a hippie haven inside, and paint the outside in psychedelic colors. Manson has the girls, in unison, chant, "Road trip," and the games are about to begin.

While San Francisco is the perfect recruiting ground for his hippie cult, the glitz and glamour of Los Angeles seems a more likely location from which to launch Helter Skelter. After a circuitous route initially takes them north to Washington, then south all the way to Mexico, they finally land in L.A. by the end of the year.

The centerpiece of the Helter Skelter philosophy is a race war from which the Manson Family will emerge as the only surviving white people. Helter Skelter is to be initiated by arranging for a group of high society white folks to become the victims of a wave of bloody murders. The upper crust white folks will naturally blame "blackie", which is the singular term Manson uses to collectively identify all black people in general.

The whites will head into the ghettos to extract revenge enraging the blacks who will launch a revolution. The retribution of blackie will lead to an all-out racial civil war. Contributing to the chaos will be the developing rift between those whites who have compassion for the blacks and those who don't. That infighting amongst the whites will weaken their race to the point where the blackie will emerge victorious, eliminating the whites from society.

While this chaos is reigning, the Manson Family will survive the massacre by hiding in a cave under Death Valley. Once Blackie assumes control of the government, they will not be competent enough to run things, thus making imminent the collapse of the black society.

At this point Manson and his followers will emerge from their cave to be blessed with an exultant reception from Blackie who can now breathe a collective sigh of relief, grateful that they once again have white people to run their lives. We just can't see what could possibly go wrong with this plan.

A year and a half after his release, when Manson delivers his New Year's Eve prophecy, he speaks of the Beatles as the soul and part of the hole in the infinite. Yeah, we know, on the surface it doesn't seem to make a lot of sense but it doesn't seem to matter. When he passionately delivers his Helter Skelter speech around the campfire at the ranch in Death Valley, his Family members buy into it completely.

Years later in his autobiography, Manson's right-hand man Tex Watson wrote, "At that point Charlie's credibility seemed indisputable. For weeks he had been talking of revolution, prophesizing it. We had listened to him rap; we were geared for it—making music to program the young love. Then, from across the Atlantic, the hottest music group on the planet substantiates Charlie with an album which is almost blood-curdling in its depiction of violence. It was uncanny." The above refers to the Beatles' *White Album.*

There's a bit of quirky story behind the title of that album. Let's seize the moment and share the explanation. It was a double album that came out in late 1967 and the official title was "The Beatles". At first glance the cover appears to be nothing but a white square, but upon closer inspection one notices the two words "The BEATLES" embossed in letters about an inch high.

Over time the title of "The White Album" became the consensus choice of how to refer to that particular album because if you were discussing the group's records and a comment was made about "The Beatles" album it might be unclear as to which album you were referring. So for the purposes of this storyline, we are heretofore defaulting to "The White Album".

The Beatles second most influential album upon Manson was *Magical Mystery Tour.* Another Family member turned author was Paul Watkins who wrote a book called *My Life With Charles Manson.* Because he is not involved in any crime, Watkins never goes to jail and subsequently is able to interview Manson for his book. In it Watkins writes, "Manson said the Beatles album *Magical Mystery Tour* expressed the essence of his own philosophy. Basically, Charlie's trip was to program us all to submit: to give up our egos, which, in a spiritual sense, is a lofty aspiration. As rebels within a materialistic, decadent culture, we could dig it." For the record, at this point we would like to add that

"Magical Mystery Tour" also happens to be a nickname given by the Family to their 1967-68 bus tour. Magic indeed!

Next we're going to take a look at some specific Beatles songs. We'll examine some lyrics and we will explain how Charlie took the words of John, Paul, George and Ringo and managed to weave them into a web of support for his Helter Skelter race war prophesy. When Manson delivered his New Year's Eve speech where he fully explained his theory and the connection to the Beatles' lyrics, they played *The White Album* over and over. But there were five songs in particular that Manson considered to be the centerpiece of the connection between his Family and the most popular rock band in the world. We'll lead with those five.

BLACKBIRD ~ This track from *The White Album* plays right into Manson's hand for two reasons. It uses the word "rise" which is go-to terminology repeated by Charlie. It is one of the words written in blood on the wall at the LaBianca murders. And if you equate "blackbird" with the black race, then you have a clear interpretation of the blacks rising up to overtake the whites.

Actually, Manson isn't completely wrong in his analysis here. Paul McCartney wrote the song in support of the African American women involved in the Civil Rights Movement of the 1960's. Lyrics include. "Blackbird singing in the dead of night/Take these broken wings and learn to fly/All your life/You were only waiting for this moment to arise." The final line in the song is, "Blackbird fly into the light of the dark black night."

HELTER SKELTER ~ This one has the added significance of serving as the title Charles Manson has bestowed upon his prophecy of the impending Armageddon resulting in the racial war that will turn the world upside down. When Manson addresses the Family on New Year's Eve 1968, he says, "Are you hep to what the Beatles are saying? Helter Skelter is coming down. The Beatles are telling it like it is."

There was an underground saying in vogue at the time which goes "The shit is coming down." It basically means all Hell is breaking loose in the sense that the bourgeois establishment is going to be brought down by the crusaders of reform. Manson often uses the "shit is coming down" phrase to describe his prophecy. When the Beatles record this song using the phrase "Helter Skelter" to replace the word "shit" it meshes perfectly with Charlie's purposes. The Beatles are merely restating what Manson has been saying all along.

According to Manson, as has been stated, his followers will escape the violence of Helter Skelter by hiding out underground in Death Valley. When the Beatles say "Look out/Helter Skelter/She's coming down fast/Yes she is," the implication is that the upcoming explosion of race-based violence is coming soon; Helter Skelter is imminent.

> *Manson had one clear philosophy*
> *Based on one aberrant prophecy*
> *That summer will swelter*
> *And bring Helter Skelter*
> *Resulting in tragic atrocity*

PIGGIES ~ In "Piggies," the piggies equal the establishment. Manson's favorite part of the song is verse 3 when the piggies are, "Living piggy lives/You can see them out for dinner/With their piggy wives/Clutching forks and knives/To eat their bacon." The song goes on to say about the piggies that, "What they need's a damn good whacking." The interpretation of this one is pretty obvious. The establishment needs to get whacked. Regarding the cutlery mentioned in the song, it should also be noted that Leno LaBianca is left with a fork in his throat and a knife in his stomach.

REVOLUTION 1 ~ This one hinges on a single word which does not even appear on the lyrics sheet included in the album. The chorus goes like this, "You say you want a revolution/Well you know we all want to change the world/But when you talk about destruction/Don't you know that you can count me out (in)." Those two little letters "in" can effectively serve to change the entire meaning. While they do not appear on the lyric sheet, they are clearly audible.

The song was credited to Lennon-McCartney, as were all songs written by John Lennon and/or Paul McCartney during their tenure with the Beatles. This one was actually written by Lennon, so let's defer to him for the actual meaning of the "out/in" lyrics/vocals. His explanation was that, after finishing the song, he was truly conflicted about violent vs. peaceful efforts to effect reform; hence, he chose to intentionally leave multiple interpretations possible.

But for Manson it is obvious how he will spin it to adapt the lyrics to his Helter Skelter philosophy. And in terms of his efforts to convince his followers that the Beatles are actually talking to them, this track is a gold mine.

Not only can he construe the words to mean the Beatles are reaching out, it could actually be presented in the context that the Beatles are asking to hear back from the Manson Family. Manson preaches that, in the song, when the Beatles say, "You say you got a real solution/Well you know, we'd all love to see the plan," they are asking the Manson Family to explain to them how Helter Skelter is going to work.

Manson uses this to bolster his position that the Family is destined to release an album supporting and validating their philosophy… the Beatles want Manson to record the album and tell them how to escape the impending horrors.

REVOLUTION 9 ~ This was the track on *The White Album* that Manson deems to be the most significant, a comment that might seem surprising when it's noted that there are no true lyrics. The track is an audio collage of over eight minutes with psychedelic instrumentation and, best of all for Manson, some audible but muddled voices hidden beneath the surface. It's a cacophony of synthesizers, horns, drums and various other sounds including machine gun fire and the oinking of pigs. You can't sing along to this one.

We played this through multiple times so that if you would like to play along with us, we can direct you to the exact spots in the track where the spoken words we refer to can be heard. At 2:18 into the track, there is a voice that seems to say, "lots of stab wounds." Manson said that this was the Beatles telling them the means by which to commit the killings which would incite Helter Skelter.

Manson's crew obviously has a gun at the Tate murders because they shoot Steven Parent as he attempts to drive away, as well as shooting Jay Sebring and Voytek Frykowski when they get inside. But to achieve

Manson's goal of making the murders "witchy," 102 stab wounds and bloody writing on the wall is certainly more gruesomely impactful.

Always the ultimate spin doctor, Manson seizes upon a segment that begins at 2:33 where a word that sounds like "rise" is repeated multiple times. The word "rise" is a cornerstone to Manson's Helter Skelter philosophy. It means that the blacks are going to rise up and kill the whites. "Rise" is one of the words painted in blood on the wall at the LaBianca murders.

At approximately 3:45 into the track, Manson points out a segment where he hears someone whispering, "Charlie, Charlie, send us a telegram." At that point there is a voice, which sounds like George Harrison to us, that does indeed seem to be talking about a telegram.

Finally, Manson gives particular relevance to the number 9 chant heard for the first time at the 11 second mark. The one part of the Bible that Manson uses most often in his preaching about Helter Skelter is Chapter 9 of the "Book of Revelation." This is a logical approach on his part because that book refers to the final apocalypse. Furthermore, "Revelation," Chapter 9, Verse 2 speaks of the "bottomless pit" which Manson equates to the underground sanctuary to which the Family plans to retreat during Helter Skelter.

So, as Charles Manson summarizes the connection between the Beatles, his Family and Helter Skelter, this track is the cherry on top. Charlie is prophesizing a revolution on the highest level. Helter Skelter is to be the greatest revolution in human history. The "Book of Revelation" features the Bible's apocalypse. And Chapter 9 of "Revelation" alludes to the bottomless pit in which the Manson Family will hide during his apocalypse.

This track is an audio expression of the coming conflict. As the Beatles repeatedly chant "Number 9" they are referring to chapter 9 in the "Book of Revelation." In the mind of Manson, Revolution 9 equals Revelation 9. The titles reflect an eerie similarity which is confirmed by the numbers being exactly equal. How crazy is that?

Even to us just sipping some wine, by our fireplace, in Mendon, Manson's ability to connect the dots is eerily effective. We're thinking that listening to Charlie preach if you were a kid, doing LSD, by a campfire in Death Valley, the effect could be easily electrifying.

> *The race wars are coming our way*
> *That's a fact I must truly convey*
> *You can take it from me*
> *Or if that just can't be*
> *Let the Beatles confirm what I say*

BUBBLING UNDER THE HOT FIVE ~ Having completed our analysis of the five songs around which Manson makes his strongest connection between his Helter Skelter theory and the music of the Beatles, we will now share with you the other Beatles tunes which Manson uses to effectively augment his argument.

BLUE JAY WAY ~ This track, written by George Harrison, is from the *Magical Mystery Tour* album. Lyrics include, "There's a fog upon LA/and my friends have lost their way/We'll be over soon they said." Manson uses these to confirm that the Beatles know where his Family is and the Beatles will be joining the Mansons soon.

CRY BABY CRY ~ This one is quirky in that it seems to portend the New Year's Eve 1968 Family gathering around the fire in Death Valley to partake of Charlie's profound premonitions about what the future holds for his children.

The Beatles sing, "At twelve o'clock a meeting 'round the table/For a séance in the dark/With voices out of nowhere/Put on specially by the children for a lark." Happy New Year!

HAPPINESS IS A WARM GUN ~ Manson's interpretation of this one is that the Beatles are telling blacks to get guns and start a race war with the whites. Some sample lyrics are, "When I hold you in my arms/And I feel my finger on your trigger/I know nobody can do me no harm/Because happiness is a warm gun." Repeated multiple times throughout the song is the chant "bang, bang, shoot, shoot."

HONEY PIE ~ This one ties into Manson's belief that the Beatles are calling upon the Family to record music which will advise the Beatles of how they can be empowered to help Manson initiate Helter Skelter. The key lyrics in this song are, "Oh honey pie/My position is tragic/Come and show me the magic/Of your Hollywood song." As Charlie interprets this, the most significant component is that the Beatles know the Family is in the Los Angeles area. But it does become doubly effective when the Beatles seem to ask the Mansons to show them the magic of the Family's music.

I WILL ~ The interpretation of this one is that the Beatles are telling the Family to record an album to advise the group of how they can assist in the precipitation of Helter Skelter. The key lyrics in this song are, "And when at last I find you/Your song will fill the air/Sing it loud so I can hear you/Make it easy to be near you/For the things you do endear you to me/You know/I will."

ROCKY RACCOON ~ In order to use the song "Rocky Raccoon" within Manson's philosophy of Helter Skelter you have to shorten the word "raccoon" to just "coon" and use it in the sense of a derogatory reference to a black person. We live in Rochester, New York. Ironically as we write this, in January of 2019, a local meteorologist in our town was recently fired for using the word "coon" in a reference to our city's Martin Luther King Jr. Park. He said it was an accident. Some accidents prove costly.

When interviewed in jail, Manson offers the following interpretation of "Rocky Raccoon." "Coon," he explains, "You know that's a word they use for black people. You know the line, 'Gideon checked out/And left no doubt/To help good Rocky's revival.' Rocky's revival – it means coming back to life. The black man is going to come into power again. 'Gideon checks out' means that it's all written out there in the Book of Revelation in the Bible."

SEXY SADIE ~ In terms of Manson convincing the Family that the Beatles are speaking through him, this one is big. But it's primarily just dumb luck. Susan Atkins, one of only three female Family members to go to jail for the murders, had been nicknamed "Sadie Mae" by Manson early on in the Family's history. The prevalent use of nicknames is part of Manson's magical mystique, but the fact that Susan Atkins' personality and body so jived with the Beatles "Sexy Sadie" song serves Manson well.

Manson Family member Tex Watson wrote that "the words of "Sexy Sadie" fit Susan Atkins so well that it made us all sure the Beatles had to be singing directly to us." Watson specifically noted that the song's title character Sadie "came along and turned on everyone," "broke the rules," and "laid it down for all to see." Tex Watson said that Sexy Sadie had broken all the rules sexually, and liked to talk about her multiple experiences and lack of inhibitions. In San Francisco, where she met Manson, Sexy Sadie had been a topless dancer.

YOU NEVER GIVE ME YOUR MONEY ~ This is the only track from the Beatles' *Abbey Road* album which seems to be specifically referenced by the Manson Family. The sparsity of *Abbey Road* references is not surprising because the album is not released until September 1969 which of course is after the murders had taken place. When the police raid Spahn Ranch on November 25, 1969 they confiscate a door upon which is written "Helter Skelter is coming down fast," and the words "1, 2, 3, 4, 5, 6, 7, all good children go to heaven." Those words are heard in "You Never Give Me Your Money" beginning at the 3:15 mark and they are repeated through the fade out.

When Manson Family member Paul Watkins wrote his book *My Life With Charles Manson*, he wrote that Manson "spent hours quoting and interpreting Revelation to the Family, particularly verses from chapter 9." Manson's right-hand man, Tex Watson said that, apart from Chapter 9 of the Book of Revelation, the Bible had "absolutely no meaning in our life in the Family." Even so, Watson stated that "we... knew that Charlie was Jesus Christ".

In working on this project, we have been toggling back and forth between Charles Manson's websites, YouTube recordings of the Beatles, and our family Bible. How's that for a crazy combination? Based upon our collaborative research, here is our biblical analysis of the preaching and philosophy of Charles Manson.

At this point we are going to segue from Manson's infatuation with the Beatles to how he manages to connect his Helter Skelter prophecy to the Bible, and have the Bible serve to validate the prophecy. As we researched this piece a continuing conundrum confounding us was how in the world Manson managed to maintain maniacal control over his faithful flock. Not that the whole thing is ever going to make complete sense on any level, but the following quote is one that stuck in our minds.

Linking the Beatles and the Bible, and using his ability to speak like a Pope, Charlie at one peak point profoundly pontificates the following. Manson says, "Look at the Beatles songs: songs sung all over the world by the young; it ain't nothin' new. It's written in Revelation, all about the four angels programming the holocaust. The four angels (the Beatles) looking for the fifth angel (Manson) to lead the people into the pit of fire, right out to Death Valley. It's all in black and white, in *The White Album*—white, so there ain't no mistakin' the color."

Okay, right now we're thinking all of you are pondering the potential possibilities. "Do I: #1) Go grab my Bible, or #2) Go grab my college yearbook and see if that last tab of acid I left on page 69 is still there?"

From the beginning it's been our policy to be upfront with our readers. If at this point, you've gone for your Bible we applaud that pedagogical pursuit. We have pulled out our Bible so many times in the writing of this Bonus Chapter it's almost difficult to gauge the number. Right now, as wife Deb queries husband Tim about how many times we've pulled out the Bible, he throws out a guestimate of 969.

Wife Deb responds by saying, "Is that actually a guess or your fantasy of a new sexual position?" When it comes to sex, we're sure you've all visualized the typical 69, but now we're sure we have your fantasy wheels spinning. What exactly would a 969 look like? And would you like us to start an online sign-up list?

And finally, Tim wants to go on record as saying that "969" guess had more to do with the Bible than with sex. Deb is thinking, "I know he's good, but what in the world is my husband going to come up with to somehow link 969 and the Bible?"

His answer… "All of this Bible reading we've been doing has got me wondering if we're going to be blessed with long life. If I could pick a lifetime to match anybody in the Bible I would go with Methuselah who lived to be 969 years old." Just when Deb thinks she's got him on the ropes he manages to wiggle off the hook.

We do have one final thought on this "969" conundrum. Reverting to the sexual interpretation of this number, here's our advice. Based upon personal experience, clearly the least fun position is that of the first "9."

With all of that being said, those that took the acid option above will already be fumbling to find where they left their bookmarks last night. For you Bible bearing believers, let's dutifully continue to wend our way onto the Word.

The next component of our composition is to share with you our legitimately serious biblical research analyzing Manson's use of the Book of Revelation to validate his apocalyptic proclamations. Our format will be: Bible verse followed by (Manson's interpretation.)

Chapter 7, Verse 1: The apostle John says, "And after these things I saw four angels… and I saw another angel ascending… and he cried with a loud voice to the four angels." (Interpretation: The four angels are the Beatles and Charles Manson is the fifth angel.)

Chapter 9, Verse 1: Then the fifth angel sounded, and I saw a star from heaven which had fallen to the earth; and the key of the bottomless pit was given to him. (Interpretation: As the fifth angel, Manson took this line to mean the Beatles would be joining his Family. The "bottomless pit" was the underground cave in Death Valley to which the Family would escape and hide during Helter Skelter.)

Verse 3: Then out of the smoke came locusts upon the earth, and power was given them. (Interpretation: Locusts are, in fact, beetles, so this one is pretty easy. The locusts equal the Beatles.)

Verse 4: And it was commanded them that they should not hurt the grass of the earth, neither any green thing, neither any tree. (Interpretation: Perhaps surprisingly, while Manson's philosophies allowed for the killing of humans, he opposed the killing of plants and animals. At times he severely reprimanded Family members for killing scorpions and rattlesnakes.)

Verse 4: They were told not to hurt... men who... have the seal of God on their foreheads. (Interpretation: This fore shadows Manson, followed by the rest of his Family, carving crosses into their foreheads at the beginning of the trial.)

Verse 7 – 8: The locusts'... faces were as men's faces and they had hair like the hair of women. (Interpretation: This confirms that the locusts were men, representing the Beatles, with long hair.)

Verse 9: They had... breastplates of iron. (Interpretation: The breastplates of iron were the Beatles' electric guitars.)

Verse 11: They have as king over them, the angel of the abyss, whose name in the Hebrew tongue is Abaddon, but in the Greek tongue hath his name Apollyon. (Interpretation: The fifth angel, Manson, is the king of his Family and again the abyss is the underground cave in Death Valley. There is an additional irony regarding this one. The "king" also had a Latin name which, while included in the Catholic Douay Version of the Bible, was omitted in the translation of the King James Version. The king's Latin name was Exterminans which obviously and interestingly might be construed as a prophetic morphing of the words "exterminate" and "Manson.")

Verse 15: And the four angels... would kill a third of mankind. (Interpretation: This details the genocide prophesized by Manson in Helter Skelter. Manson's prophecy divides mankind into three groups, the blacks, the whites and the Manson Family. When the blacks wipe out the whites they will "kill a third of mankind.")

Verse 17: Those who... had breastplates... out of their mouths proceeded fire and smoke and brimstone. (Interpretation: Those who had breastplates were the Beatles, as established above, and the strength of their words as powerful leaders, spokesmen and prophets would ignite Helter Skelter.)

Verse 18: Mankind was killed... by the fire... and the brimstone which proceeded out of their mouths. (Interpretation: This verse essentially serves to reiterate and summarize Helter Skelter.)

Verse 20: The men... repented not of the works of their hands, that they should not worship devils, and idols of gold, and silver, and brass... neither can see, nor hear, nor walk. Mankind was killed... by the fire... and the brimstone which proceeded out of their mouths. (Interpretation: This verse essentially serves to reiterate and summarize Helter Skelter.)

Verse 21: Neither repented they of their murders, nor of their sorceries, nor of their fornications, nor of their thefts. (Interpretation: Manson chose not to make this verse part of his Bible preaching, in all likelihood because this part sounds eerily like a pinpoint description of the crimes of the Manson Family.)

So Manson probably got away with one on Verse 21, but don't we all occasionally roll the dice? Let's face it, his audience was a hippie cult, doing acid, around a campfire, on New Year's Eve, in Death Valley, in 1968. On a scale of 1-10 how high would you rate their fact checking ability? If those kids had only had internet access, Charlie would have been booed off the stage before the next joint was passed.

BONUS CHAPTER 2:
CHARACTER BACKSTORIES

CHARACTER LIST

FAMILY:

Charles Manson:	Hippie guru, king of the hill, master manipulator
Tex Watson:	Right hand man, leads Tate-LaBianca murder missions
Steve Grogan aka Clem:	On B-Team on LaBianca night, involved with murder of Shorty
Susan Atkins aka Sexy Sadie:	Involved in Tate-LaBianca murders
Linda Kasabian:	Involved in Tate-LaBianca murders, main prosecution witness
Leslie Van Houten:	Involved in LaBianca murders
Patricia Krenwinkel:	Involved in Tate-LaBianca murders
Barbara Hoyt:	Despite being dosed with LSD testifies against Family
Ruth Ann Moorehouse:	Flies Barbara Hoyt to Hawaii for murder attempt
Lynette Fromme aka Squeaky:	George Spahn's sex slave, attempts to assassinate President Ford
Bobby Beausoleil:	Family member who kills Gary Hinman
Mary Brunner:	Involved in Hinman murder, bore Manson's child
Danny DeCarlo:	Family Sergeant at Arms who testifies at trial

OTHER PERIPHERAL:

William Garretson:	Lived in guest house at site of Tate murders
Dennis Wilson:	Beach Boys' drummer who connects Manson with music industry
Terry Melcher:	Record producer whose house is later occupied by Sharon Tate
George Spahn:	Owner of Spahn Ranch, film set occupied by the Family
Juan Flynn:	Spahn Ranch farmhand who testifies against the Family
Judges:	William Keene/Charles Older
Attorneys:	Anthony Bugliosi (Prosecuting), Irving Kanarek (Manson) Paul Fitzgerald (Krenwinkel), Daye Shinn (Atkins), Ronald Hughes→Maxwell Keith (Van Houten)

MURDER VICTIMS:

Gary Hinman:	Killed by Bobby Beausoleil for not giving Family money
Sharon Tate:	Actress killed by Family while 8½ months pregnant
Jay Sebring:	Hollywood hair stylist, victim at Tate murders
Abigail Folger:	Heir to coffee fortune, victim at Tate murders
Voytek Frykowski:	Folger's boyfriend, victim at Tate murders
Stephen Parent:	Leaving guest house, becomes victim at Tate murders
Leno & Rosemary LaBianca:	Millionaire victims of second murder spree
Donald Shea aka Shorty:	Murdered and dismembered by Family at Spahn Ranch

CHARACTER BACKSTORIES

The purpose of this Bonus Chapter is to supply some additional information on the various people involved with this story. Think of it as being kind of a "before and after" look at the major players. Our goal was to fill you in on personal background prior to involvement with the Manson story, and also what happened to these people after the trial ended. We have organized our biographical blurbs in the following format:

- FAMILY MEMBERS
- VICTIMS
- COURTROOM PEOPLE
- MISCELLANEOUS OTHERS

FAMILY MEMBERS
SUSAN ATKINS ~ SADIE MAE GLUTZ ~ SEXY SADIE
(1948-2009)

Susan Atkins was one of three children born to alcoholic middle-class parents in San Jose, California. As a child she was described as a quiet, self-conscious girl who was involved in various church and school activities.

She met Charles Manson when he was playing guitar at a San Francisco house she lived in with several friends. Atkins accepted his offer to hit the road for a summer tour with his Family in their newly painted hippie bus.

After the trial Susan Atkins led a fairly productive and positive life in prison becoming a born-again Christian in 1974. While incarcerated, Atkins became involved with various prison programs including teaching classes and providing health assistance to other inmates.

Susan Atkins was married twice in prison, each marriage carrying with it a somewhat interesting side story. Her first marriage was to Donald Lee Laisure in 1981 and Laisure was one frisky fellow. Atkins was his 35th wife. As one might have predicted, this one didn't stand the test of time; it wasn't long until Laisure leisurely moved on to #36.

She did much better her second time around in 1987, marrying a Harvard Law School graduate named James W. Whitehouse who was fifteen years younger than her. Whitehouse would end up representing her in subsequent parole hearings and maintaining a website dedicated to her release. He would remain married to her until her death.

Susan Atkins was denied parole nineteen times and when she died in 2009, she was the longest-serving female inmate in the California penal system.

BOBBY BEAUSOLEIL ~ CUPID
(1947-   )

Bobby Beausoleil was born into a middle class Catholic family in Santa Barbara, California. He had a rather rocky youth and was sentenced to ten months at Los Prietos Boys Camp when he was just 15 years old. Drawn to music and acting, he became involved in the California counterculture scene.

In 1968, he scored the role of the title character in the film *Lucifer Rising*, the biggest of four movies in which he appeared, and he also played in multiple rock bands during the mid-to-late '60's. After meeting Manson in 1968, Charlie was anxious to add a good-looking actor and musician into the fold and Beausoleil was successfully recruited into the Family.

The Beausoleil story, after incarceration, actually possesses a stunning amount of depth. He is a truly talented musician and visual artist. Over the years he has recorded nine albums and his artwork has been displayed in multiple galleries.

Probably his most notable musical achievement was writing and recording the soundtrack to the *Lucifer Rising* film while he was in prison. Director Kenneth Anger decided he wanted to add a soundtrack to the film and after hearing some music that Beausoleil had composed for this project, Anger recruited him to write the entire soundtrack, a project that was completed in 1980.

That was the first of Beausoleil's nine commercially released albums spanning the last three decades and all of his material has received generally very good critical review. The 2019 Lady Gaga Netflix documentary called *Gaga: Five Foot Two* features three tracks by Beausoleil including "Lucifer Rising".

And that wasn't even his best news of the year. On January 3, 2019, a California parole board recommended Beausoleil be freed. In the recommendation it was stated that "during his nearly half-century of incarceration he had devoted himself to creativity and pro-social growth, gradually maturing into, at this present age of 71, a person exhibiting compassion and empathy."

LYNETTE FROMME ~ SQUEAKY
(1948-   )

Lynette Fromme was born into an upper middle class family in Santa Monica, California, the daughter of an aeronautical engineer. Especially when you combine the saga of Manson Family members both before and after the Tate-LaBianca era, Squeaky has the hands-down best storyline.

While in grade school she became a member of a dance group called the Westchester Lariats. The Lariat lassies went on to achieve considerable success appearing both on the *Lawrence Welk Show* and at the White House. Of course the ultimate irony of the White House appearance would be that 25 years later she would try to assassinate President Gerald Ford.

How's that for an encore performance? Perhaps if she'd worn her old Westchester Lariat uniform to the assassination attempt, she might have been able to maneuver herself into a more advantageous position to commit the crime.

After her prestigious elementary school years enabled her to dance in distant locations as far away as Europe, Lynette's high school experience unfortunately dropped her into a sobering sinkhole, or perhaps not-so-sobering would be a better way to describe it. Before her graduation in 1966 she had succumbed to a persistent use of drugs and alcohol.

Enter Charlie. In 1967 Lynette met Charles Manson at Venice Beach and was enticed into joining the Family as one of its earliest and youngest members. Her role would remain significant throughout the course of the Family history. This fact would be validated during the time of the trial, the most high profile era in Manson Family history.

With Charlie and the others in prison, moving forward, the Family needed a new public face and spokesperson, a new head honcho so to speak. Without any specific plan in place as to who would assume that role, Squeaky managed to slide right into it. She was cute, she was glib, and as the Manson disciples and reporters continued to circulate and comingle on the courthouse steps, Squeaky became everybody's go-to gal.

In terms of a long range storyline, Squeaky also had the advantage that, as opposed to Susan Atkins, Patricia Krenwinkel and Leslie Van Houten, she had not been a participant in the Tate-LaBianca murders. Deferring to the dreaded *Monopoly* dictum, she would not be told to "Go directly to jail, Do not pass Go, Do not collect $200".

Of course this advantage proved short-lived. Turns out that "Go directly to jail" card would be cashed in by Squeaky just a few years down the road. Having established her monopoly on Boardwalk and Park Place, Squeaky decided that the next most logical move would be to try and kill the president.

Switching board game motifs from *Monopoly* to *Clue*, Squeaky's strategy was to go to Sacramento's Capitol Park where President Ford was speaking and have the murder play out as follows. It would be committed "By Lynette Fromme, With the revolver, In the park." Okay, admittedly, we are breaking some of the standards of traditional board game rules, but let's face it, aren't we all just having fun here? We haven't actually killed anybody yet, have we?

At any rate, here's the scoop on how Squeaky managed to squander her get out of jail card. On September 5, 1975, dressed in a red robe, she went to Capitol Park to plead for the plight of the California redwoods. Nice cause and all, but as we assess this project, in retrospect, we would like to have made the following basic suggestion to Squeaky.

We would have said, "Squeaky, it's all about the wardrobe, girl. We know red is your color, matches your hair and all. We also know you look good in robes, and we do support, in principle, your drive to protect the California redwoods. That being said, there are two possible outcomes from your wearing the red robe."

"One would be that President Ford will notice your robe from a distance, become inspired by the symbolism (red robe = redwoods, we get it), and the president will come to truly embrace the environmental cause. There's a little bit of tree-hugger in all of us."

"The second possibility is that the Secret Service will see your red robe as a red flag and be even more likely to notice the pointed object protruding from under the robe. So, Squeaky, to conclude the wardrobe portion of this lecture, in selecting the most advantageous apparel for attempting an assassination, the choice of the bright red robe was probably not very well thought out on your part."

After her apprehension, Squeaky turned her trial into an adventure. She refused to cooperate with her attorney, basically assuring she would receive the maximum penalty of life in prison. When the prosecuting attorney said she was "full of hate and violence" Squeaky threw an apple at him scoring a direct hit to the face which knocked his glasses off. Hopefully the scouts for the prison baseball team were in the audience!

After receiving her life sentence, Squeaky left the courtroom with some memorable words. She said, " I came to get life. Not just my life but clean air, healthy water, and respect for creatures and creation." Feel free to quote her on that if you like.

If you're thinking the life sentence would pretty much end the story for the Squeakster, you're going to have to stand corrected. While serving time at the Federal Correctional Institution for Women in Alderson, West Virginia, she escaped on Christmas Eve 1987. She managed to spend her entire Christmas Day as a free woman before being recaptured on December 26. No word on what Santa left in her stocking.

Then, fast forwarding, she was actually released on parole on August 14, 2009. What has Squeaky been up to since reclaiming her freedom? Well, we've got good news and bad news. The good news is she hasn't tried to kill anybody. The bad news is there's now a house in New York State totally covered with painted skeletons.

Lynette is living with her boyfriend Robert Valdner, himself paroled for a 1988 manslaughter charge. Apparently, "I slept with Charles Manson," is not as lame of a pickup line as you might think it would be. If you happen to be passing through central New York and want to stop for a visit, heading toward Utica it's a house in Marcy, NY, the one decorated with the aforementioned painted skulls. It's Halloween 365 days a year at the Fromme household.

LINDA KASABIAN ~ LINDA CHRISTIAN
(1949-   )

Linda Kasabian was raised in Milford, New Hampshire in a financially struggling middle class home. Her father left, her mother remarried and she ended up the oldest of several children in a situation where her mother acknowledged that she had too many children and stepchildren to do a good job with Linda.

People described young Linda as being intelligent, kind and shy, but long-story-short, she had to grow up too fast. Kasabian ran away from home at 16 and had a husband and child by the time she was 17. She followed her husband to California and when he took off, she found herself drawn into the L.A. hippie hangouts.

At one of these she ran into Catherine "Gypsy" Share who enticed her to visit Spahn Ranch and experience the idyllic lifestyle prevalent there. Assured by Manson and his followers that she and her daughter would be welcomed and protected, she decided to stay.

After the trial, Kasabian returned to her roots in New Hampshire and has led a relatively quiet life, raising her two daughters there, and staying out of the spotlight, for the most part.

PATRICIA KRENWINKEL ~ KATIE ~ MARNIE REEVES
(1947-   )

Patricia Krenwinkel grew up in a middle class household in Los Angeles. She suffered from low self-esteem in school and was often bullied because of her weight.

She originally considered becoming a nun and to that end spent a semester at Spring Hill College, a Jesuit school in Alabama. But she baled on that plan and returned to California where she ran into Charles Manson at Manhattan Beach in 1967 and went on to become a part of the Family.

Originally, upon her incarceration, Krenwinkel remained loyal to Manson and the Family but that gradually changed to the point where she would eventually disavow everything Manson. Her prison resumé is particularly perky.

In addition to earning a college degree, she plays guitar, writes music, and is even on the prison volleyball team. Her pristine prison record includes volunteer work with Alcoholics Anonymous and Narcotics Anonymous and she has also given her time teaching inmates everything from dance lessons to literacy.

Now at the California Institution for Women in Chino, she has been denied parole 14 times. As of this writing, Krenwinkel is the longest-serving female inmate in California.

CHARLES MANSON
(1934-2017)

We've covered Manson's early years in the main portion of the book, so at this point we will just share the highlights of his life after the trial. Because of his high profile, it's perhaps surprising that Manson lived to an old age in the prison system. By comparison, Jeffrey Dahmer only lasted three years.

That being said, Manson's later years were not a prison picnic. He was sodomized by sophisticated prison organizations such as the Aryan Nation, as well as being victimized by lone wolf Jan Holmstrom who poured paint thinner on Charlie and lit him on fire following Charlie's complaints about his Hare Krishna chants. Talk about "Instant Karma" coming back to get you... the Beatles were totally into Hare Krishna.

Manson gave a handful of television interviews during his jail time. Below we will list the most significant:

1981 ~ Tom Snyder for NBC *The Tomorrow Show*
1986 ~ Charlie Rose for CBS News *Nightwatch*
1988 ~ Geraldo Rivera for *Devil Worship: Exposing Satan's Underground*
1993 ~ Diane Sawyer for *Truth and Lies: The Family Manson*

OUR HYPOTHETICAL INTERVIEW ~ Here's our funniest hypothetical interview of Manson in prison. Let's set the Wayback Machine for February of 1987 when the Beatles albums first came out on compact disc. Upon gaining access to Manson for this interview, we know how obsessed he always was with the Beatles so we decide to go to that topic first.

We ask him if he's been able to hear the Beatles rereleases in the new digital compact disc format. Charlie responds, "Yeah, and the clarity on these CD's is just ear-shattering, man. I mean you can fuckin' hear everything and I guess, in retrospect, they probably weren't really talkin' to me on the albums. I don't know if I had a blown speaker or what. God, do I feel like such an idiot! Any chance I could get a do-over on this whole mess?"

Of course there would be no do-over for Charlie. And of course there also would be no parole, that having been denied 12 times over the years. Suffering from colon cancer, Manson went into cardiac arrest and died on November 19, 2017.

LESLIE VAN HOUTEN
(1949-   )

Leslie Van Houten was born in Altadena, California into a church-going middle-class family. After her parents divorced during her middle teens, she turned to drugs, ran away from home, and became ensconced in the hippie culture of L.A.

Van Houten's first contact with Manson was through a friend, Catherine "Gypsy" Share who was also Patricia Krenwinkel's first Family contact. By the summer of 1968, Van Houten had become a regular fixture with the Manson Family at Spahn Ranch.

Of the four Manson Family members convicted at the first trial, Leslie Van Houten was the only one who would ever experience freedom again, albeit for only a brief period of time. In 1977, she was granted a retrial based on the argument that when her original lawyer died during the trial, a mistrial should have been declared in her case. So she was actually out on bail for six months for that retrial.

There was some new drama injected into Van Houten's legal plight at that point. Her retrial resulted in a hung jury necessitating yet another, third trial for her. The third trial resulted in the guilty verdict being reinstated and Van Houten was returned to prison.

By 2013 Van Houten's appeals for parole had been rejected exactly 20 times by the State of California. But just when you think the drama is over, it's not. On September 6, 2017, a judicial panel recommended parole stating that Van Houten had "radically changed her life in the more than 40 years she has been incarcerated". At that point Governor Jerry Brown denied the parole, which he had the power to do.

But this one may not be over yet. On January 30, 2019, Van Houten was once again recommended for parole, and as of that point California had a new lead official. As of this writing, Governor Gavin Newsom has recently denied the parole recommendation.

CHARLES WATSON ~ TEX
(1945-   )

Charles Watson grew up in a very normal rural Texas environment. He was born in the small town of Farmersville and raised in nearby Copeville, as the youngest of three children. His high school resumé was stellar; his accomplishments including National Honor Society, editor of the school paper, and lettering in multiple sports.

He subsequently graduated from the University of North Texas where he joined a fraternity. The frat, in and of itself, probably wouldn't be worth mentioning except for one thing. After graduating he took a job at Braniff International where one of his perks was free airline tickets. Taking advantage of this, Watson flew to L.A. to visit a fraternity brother. It was during this visit that he made the connection to Manson and joined the Family.

After his incarceration Watson became a born-again Christian in 1975, and an ordained minister in 1981. He also married Kristin Joan Svege in 1979, and through conjugal visits Watson fathered a family of four children. The couple divorced in 2003. Watson earned a B.S. in business management through California Coast University in 2009. He has been denied parole 17 times.

VICTIMS
ABIGAIL FOLGER
(1943-1969)

Abigail Folger was born with the proverbial silver spoon in her mouth, daughter of coffee magnate Peter Folger. She graduated from

Radcliff with honors. Abigail was an artsy girl, into books and poetry, and her college resumé lists her performances in several plays.

In 1964, she enrolled in Harvard and got a second degree in art history. Returning home she went to work at the University of California's art museum in Berkeley as publicity director. Bored with California she left for New York City in 1967.

In the Big Apple she worked for a magazine distributor. Jobs for Abigail were just a way to keep busy, as opposed to a means of supporting herself. Her Folger inheritance paid her $130,000 per year, an amount which translates to slightly over a million dollars a year by today's standards.

In January 1968, she met Voytek Frykowski, the man who would become the love of the rest of her life. Of course the rest of that life would not prove to be very long. In August they decided to move to L.A. where Frykowski could pursue his ambition to become a screenwriter while Folger could pursue her interests in various charities.

They rented a home on a hill in Laurel Canyon across the street from Cass Elliott of the Mamas and Papas. "California Dreaming" was indeed becoming a reality. The couple moved into the Polanski-Tate home on April 1, 1969, ostensibly to housesit while Roman and Sharon were away on various film projects. They lived in the glamour of Hollywood's high society, which the media referred to as the "beautiful people."

On the evening of August 8, 1969, the beautiful people had dinner at one of L.A.'s ritziest restaurants, El Coyoté. It would be their last supper. The beautiful people returned home around 10:00 pm and began to live out the last few hours of their lives.

VOYTEK FRYKOWSKI
(1936-1969)

Voytek Frykowski was born in Poland in 1936, the son of a textile printer. Ironically, Frykowski crossed paths with Roman Polanski when they were both kids in Krakow, and the details of their first meeting make for a good story because their initial encounter would not have forebode fast friendship in the future.

Polanski was working the door at a school dance and was told that Frykowski was a troublemaker who was not to be allowed in. Frykowski did try to get into the dance and when Polanski stood his ground and forbade entrance, the two almost came to blows.

Some time later they happened to cross paths at a bar, Voytek bought Roman a drink, and the two ended up hitting it off, primarily due to a mutual interest in filmmaking. In 1961 Frykowski financed and produced an early short film Polanski made called *Mammals*. Polanski would later tell stories of some hard drinking nights out that were shared by the pair while still in Poland.

Frykowski left Poland in 1967 and, after spending some time in Paris, he moved to the United States. In New York he met Abigail Folger and even though Frykowski couldn't speak much English, the two hit it off. They both happened to be fluent in French so that became the "official language" of the relationship, with Frykowski eventually adding English to his skill set. After living together in New York for a few months, the pair decided to move to California in August of 1968.

Originally renting their L.A. house, as described in the previous Folger bio, the couple eventually moved into the Polanski-Tate home. The Frykowski-Folger relationship had begun to deteriorate by the summer of 1968 and what the future might hold for them was somewhat up in the air. Those questions would all be answered in short order on the evening of August 8, just after midnight.

JAY SEBRING
(1933-1969)

Jay Sebring was Hollywood's most renown men's hair stylist of the 1960's. He was absolutely the stylist of the stars. In a decade that began with the most well-known advertising line in men's hair products being "Brylcreem, a little dab'll do ya", Sebring would change the course of men's grooming styles forever. By the end of the decade, for the first time in the history of hair, rather than greasing down their coifs, men were using blow dryers and hair spray.

The degree to which Sebring ran with the Hollywood elite was, to say at least, impressive. Based in L.A., he flew to Las Vegas every three weeks to style the hair of Frank Sinatra and Sammy Davis Jr. At home his client list included movie stars and musicians such as Warren Beatty, Steve McQueen, and the Doors' Jim Morrison. Sebring was particularly proud of the long flowing locks he styled to enhance Morrison's cutting edge image.

Sebring had a few acting cameo appearances, always appearing as a barber or hair stylist. Our favorite was the 1965 episode of the classic *Batman* TV series when he was held captive by Catwoman. In the typical style of the campy crime-comedy they punned with his character name. Rather than being called Mr. "Sebring", he was called Mr. "Oceanbring". If you were at all unsure about how to pronounce his name, that should clear any confusion; the first syllable was pronounced like the word "sea".

In 1964, Sebring met Sharon Tate and the two began a relationship. That ended however in 1966 when Tate went to England to work on the film *The Fearless Vampire Killers* which was being directed by Roman Polanski. Enamored of him, Tate broke off her relationship with Sebring to begin one with Polanski. Despite the awkward ending to the relationship, Sebring and Tate remained friends to the very end, literally.

SHARON TATE
(1943-1969)

Sharon Tate's early life was spent as that of a military brat, no condescension intended whatsoever, but by the time she was 16 Sharon had lived in six different cities. And there were some awards to be won along the way. As she would eventually compile her modeling resumé, always appearing chronologically at the top of the list would be the fact that at the age of 6 months she won the "Miss Tiny Tot of Dallas Pageant".

Her father, Army officer Colonel Paul James Tate, was a no-nonsense guy who certainly never envisioned modeling or acting in his daughter's future. But sometimes the dominoes go down in directions dictated by destiny. And sometimes demanding dictatorial Dads just don't matter. Entering her first beauty pageant in 1959, Sharon was crowned "Miss Richland" as the queen of the high school she was attending in Richland, Washington.

Primed to compete for the state's title of "Miss Washington", those pageantry plans were permanently postponed by Colonel Tate's receiving orders to be stationed in Verona, Italy. How's this for an opportunity for a little Shakespearean irony to kick in? Colonel Tate just happened to bring his beautiful daughter to the Italian city which served as the setting for *Romeo and Juliet*. (We're sure there's a Roman Polanski joke bouncing around here somewhere, after all Juliet was only 13 years old, the same age as the girl Polanski pleaded guilty to raping in 1977).

While in Verona, Tate pursued some modeling opportunities and found herself a local celebrity after landing on the cover page of a military magazine called Stars and Stripes. Subsequently, during her Italian escape, Sharon found out that in nearby Vicenza an American movie was being filmed called *Hemingway's Adventures of a Young Man,* starring Paul Newman, Susan Strasberg and Richard Beymer. Beymer, for those of you too young to remember, played Tony in *West Side Story*. Tate went to the movie set, met Beymer, and the two ended up dating during their time together in Italy.

So, fulfilling our previous promise to provide some Shakespearean Sharon Tate irony, here we go. She comes with her father to Verona, Italy which was the setting of Shakespeare's *Romeo and Juliet*. The basic premise of *West Side Story* was to take the plot of *Romeo and Juliet* and transfer it to a modern-day New York City setting with feuding street gangs replacing the feuding families. Richard Beymer's character of Tony in *West Side Story* is the equivalent of Romeo in *Romeo and Juliet*. So, Sharon Tate comes to the setting of Romeo and finds her Romeo, so to speak.

While still in Italy, Beymer connects Tate with Pat Boone and facilitates an appearance of Sharon Tate on *The Pat Boone Chevy Showroom*, a U.S. variety show that was filming an episode in Venice at the time.

In 1962, Colonel Tate moved his family back to Los Angeles where daughter Sharon pursued acting opportunities. Here's a flashback to 1960's sitcoms to be enjoyed by all who love that genre. Tate auditioned unsuccessfully for the role of Billie Jo Bradley on *Petticoat Junction* but she did secure bit parts in *Mister Ed* and *The Beverly Hillbillies*.

Bring on 1964. This was the year that Sharon Tate met and fell in love with Jay Sebring who was a famous Hollywood hair stylist. Infatuated with Tate, Sebring proposed. Tate, however, driven by her pursuit of a film career, declined the proposal, but the two remained close until the night they would both die together.

It was also in 1964 when Sharon Tate would meet Roman Polanski during the filming of *The Fearless Vampire Killers*. It was not love at first sight. Polanski had wanted Jill St. John to play the lead role but his co-director insisted upon Sharon Tate. While Polanski was initially critical of her acting abilities, their relationship gradually improved both professionally and personally. They began to date and she moved into his apartment.

Upon completion of *Vampire Killers*, Sharon Tate's return to the states led to her next film which was *Don't Make Waves*. Inspired by the Beach Boys surf music craze, the film was a light-hearted sex-on-the-beach romp. The catch phrase espoused on the movie poster was "Turn On! Stay Loose! Make Out!" Certainly, words to live by.

The thin plot, in which Sharon played the character of "Malibu, Queen of the Beach" left little room for Tate to expand upon her acting credentials. Probably the best thing that could be said about her performance is that she looked great in a bikini. Those looks however did lead to Tate's next big payday. Her sun-baked body was featured in a major advertising campaign for Coppertone's Sunscreen tanning lotion.

Husband Roman Polanski's next big movie production project was the film *Rosemary's Baby*. Polanski had hoped to manipulate things behind the scenes to enable the lead role to be played by Tate. His efforts however proved unsuccessful and the more experienced Mia Farrow ended up starring as Rosemary.

Despite this setback, the world did seem to be taking notice of Sharon Tate. She was frequently present on the set during the filming of *Rosemary's Baby* and despite not acting in the film, when *Esquire* magazine dropped in to do a story about the movie in production, the subsequent feature had more pictures of Sharon Tate than of Mia Farrow.

The March 1967 issue of *Playboy* magazine featured Sharon Tate in a spread of nude pictures taken by Roman Polanski. The headline of the accompanying article was titled "This is the Year Sharon Tate Happens".

Things seemed to be looking up. Tate next landed the role as one of the three lead actresses, joining Patty Duke and Barbara Parkins, in the movie *Valley of the Dolls*.

This would turn out to be her final performance and making a projection on where her career might have gone is a truly enigmatic task. Let's flip a coin and we'll do the "tails" side first. Seizing upon the obvious pun, she had a great tail, but that may have been the greatest thing she had going for her.

In *Valley of the Dolls*, in what may have been an excellent example of art imitating life, Tate played the character of Jennifer North, an aspiring actress admired primarily for her body. To share one other example of this viewpoint, *Look* magazine published an article on the movie in which they described Tate as a "hopelessly stupid and vain starlet".

But reverting to our earlier imagery, there are two sides to every coin. Flipping to the "heads" side, Sharon Tate certainly had her supporters, which we will sample in the following reviews of her performance in *Valley of the Dolls*. Film director Mark Robson said about her, "Few actresses have her kind of vulnerability. She's got a great future." *The New York Times* called her performance "chillingly beautiful" and an MGM press release described her as "one of the screen's most exciting new personalities". *Newsweek* described her as "astoundingly photogenic, infinitely curvaceous," and went on to say, "Sharon Tate is one of the most smashing young things to hit Hollywood in a long time."

MISCELLANEOUS
VINCENT BUGLIOSI
(1934-2015)

Prior to his involvement with the Manson case, Vincent Bugliosi had established himself as a stellar attorney in the Los Angeles District Attorney's Office, successfully prosecuting 105 out of 106 felony trials.

Clearly his most high-profile case was that of Charles Manson and the Tate-LaBianca murders. After winning that case, Bugliosi went on to write *Helter Skelter*, his award-winning book about the trial which was published in 1974.

Amongst other books, Vincent Bugliosi also published in 1996 a book called *Outrage: The Five Reasons Why O.J. Simpson Got Away with Murder*. Back on familiar ground, the Nicole Brown/Ronald Goldman murders provided Bugliosi with a perfect podium upon which to once again expose the pitiful performance of the LAPD.

DONALD SHEA ～ SHORTY
(1933-1969)

Donald Shea was born in Massachusetts and moved to California in 1958 to pursue an acting career. He achieved only modest success in this pursuit, performing as a stuntman while also scoring bit roles in a handful of B-grade Western movies. His nickname of "Shorty" was facetious as Shea stood 6' 4" tall.

Shea's primary means of financial support was provided by his service at the Spahn Movie Ranch where his death certificate identified him as "foreman". By the time the Spahn Ranch entered the Manson story, it had become a dilapidated old movie set depicting the customary establishments one would expect to see in an old TV or movie Western. As you walked down Spahn's Main Street you would stroll by several saloons, the blacksmith shop, the sheriff's office, the post office, etc.

Shea was never enamored of the decision by his boss George Spahn to allow the Manson Family to move onto the ranch in exchange for handiwork and sexual favors. But George was the boss and with the financial options of the decaying ranch limited, Shea had little choice but accept the arrangement.

However, as the Manson Family's conflicts with the law intensified, Shea became more vocal and confrontational about the Manson crew. After the ranch was raided by police on August 16, Manson suspected Shea of having provided the police with the information needed to facilitate the raid. Shea was subsequently killed, and dismembered, by the Family on August 26, 1969. His body parts would not be discovered until 10 years later.

GEORGE SPAHN
(1889-1974)

George Spahn was the owner and operator of an old-fashioned Western film set which he rented out to film Western movies and TV shows during the 1950's and 1960's. By the end of the '60's, his ranch falling into disrepair, Spahn struck a deal with Charles Manson to allow Charlie to move his Family onto the property in return for sexual favors, provision of daily chores, and help overseeing the rental of horses for trail riding. The ranch was completely destroyed by a wildfire on September 26, 1970.

BONUS CHAPTER 3:
THE STRIKE OF THE COBRA EFFECT

UNINTENDED CONSEQUENCES ~ In this addendum we are tackling a venomous topic known as the Cobra Effect. The term stems from a specific event which we will describe here and it has come to be used in a general sense for other events which mirror the circumstances of the original Cobra Effect story. Here's a basic definition.

The Cobra Effect occurs when a seemingly logical solution to a problem ironically exacerbates the situation, resulting in the unintended consequence that the problem becomes even worse than it was before. Be honest; it's happened to all of us.

But next time it happens to you, perhaps you'll be comforted by the knowledge that the Smiths share your grief. And because of us, you can at least couch the embarrassment when explaining your faux pas to others by showing off the fact that you've mastered a cool sounding term applicable to the situation.

Here's what you do… utter the phrase "Damn Cobra Effect!" rather softly but loud enough that others in the room will hear you. This will successfully shift the focus of attention from your mistake to the inevitable question, "What's the Cobra Effect?" Now you're armed, dangerous and ready to launch into your explanation. But first you'll need a little expertise, and that's what we're here for.

SNARING THE SNAKES ~ The original Cobra Effect story goes back to British India in the mid 1800's. Obviously spoiled by the virtually total absence of poisonous tropical snakes on the streets of London, the new British governor of India was totally appalled by the fact that on his afternoon stroll to the tea stand he would occasionally encounter live cobras on the streets of the capital of Delhi (It became New Delhi in 1927).

But those Brits are brainy and brilliantly bright. And the governor came up with a bold idea which may have foreshadowed why this whole colonialism thing was destined for failure from the get-go. The British governor issued a proclamation that a bounty would be paid for every cobra skin submitted by the Indian populace. Things started out well with industrious Indians setting traps everywhere to cage and capture countless cobras.

BEATING THE SYSTEM ⁓ However, in addition to those honest industrious Indians there were also some enterprising, ingenious and illicitly inclined Indians. Seeing an obvious plan to bilk the Brits, an opportunistic group of Indians began establishing, for lack of a better term, cobra farms. Cobras breed pretty well under any circumstances but when you ploy them with soft lights, fine wine and a snake charmer playing sultry jazz, you end up with enough snake eggs to freak out the Easter Bunny. The British were shoveling out a shitload of shillings.

Of course, there was an ironic and poetic justice about the whole thing. Some of the vast quantities of money the British were exploiting from the Indians, the Indians were retrieving from the British. Fair is fair, or perhaps a better way to put it would be unfair deserves unfair. And while we're rattling off clichés, inevitably in the Indian cobra scam, all good things must come to an end.

THE GIG IS UP ⁓ When the monthly bounty payout had quintupled from the inception of the program, the British came to the realization, that their rationalization, that the Indians had just gotten really good at their snake trapping skills was probably not the case. The Indians were cheating, so the snake bounty program was terminated with the British wishing there was some kind of market for used cobra skins and the Indian snake farmers looking to book vacations to the Mediterranean.

All of this is interesting, but there's a final and inevitable piece of the story you probably haven't anticipated yet. And it's this final piece that makes the British India story the defining moment in establishing it as the namesake for the concept known as the Cobra Effect. While the rural surrounding areas of Delhi had become increasingly infested with clandestine cobra farms to cash in on the British bounty, connect the dots and predict what happens when the bounty is discontinued.

THE PLAN BACKFIRES ~ Put yourself in the place of the snake farmers. You've got a farm full of poisonous snakes and nothing to do with them. It's not like there's a reptile animal shelter down the road where you could leave them at the door. And while the best answer for humanity would be for you to kill the snakes, keep in mind that you admittedly are not one of the most ethical people in India in the first place.

Why spend your time and endanger your life in the process of killing poisonous animals when you have the option of doing nothing, letting the snakes go and just walking away from the whole mess? Ask yourself the following question… which would you rather do; risk your life killing poisonous snakes or pack your bags for that aforementioned trip to the Mediterranean?

CONFIRMING THE COBRA EFFECT ~ So inevitably all the snakes were released and of course many of them found their way back to Delhi. Long story short, the British government spent 10,000 shillings to eradicate the cobras and ended up with twice as many as they started with. And that's the original story which generated the use of the term "Cobra Effect" for any situation where a seemingly logical attempt to solve a problem results in the unintended consequence of making the problem even worse than it was before.

PARALLELS IN ENTERTAINMENT ~ There have been many manifestations of the Cobra Effect in show business.

The Last Temptation of Christ ~ In 1988 Universal Pictures released a religious drama called *The Last Temptation of Christ*. The film included a handful of departures from traditional gospel narratives including scenes where Christ is depicted as building crosses for the Romans and being tormented by the voice of God. Christian groups were generally enraged and the part that really got their nighties in a knot was where

Jesus becomes engaged and is briefly seen consummating his marriage to Mary Magdalene.

It would not seem to be the type of movie that would, in and of itself, scream "blockbuster." But the protesting religious zealots created such a clamor that box office receipts totally exceeded expectations because a lot of people who would never had considered going to a "Jesus" movie, ended up doing just that in order to see what all the ruckus was about. Damn Cobra Effect.

Barbara Streisand ~ Here's a final entertainment related example of the Cobra Effect. In 2003 Pictopia.com posted an online photograph of Barbara Streisand's coastline Malibu mansion. Suffice it to say, Babs was boisterously bitchin'. She was so sure the stalkers would soon be swimming to her shore, Streisand swiftly sued.

But to alter the lyrics to her signature song, perhaps Streisand might have been better served by telling herself, "Patience, People Who Have Patience/Are the Luckiest People in the World." Rather than just ignoring the post as a trivial inconvenience, Babs overreacted and called out the dogs on her legal team.

Here are the Streisand stats on the legal status. After her first two lawyers visited the site, they realized that the total number of hits was six, two of which were theirs. Ignoring their advice, Streisand pursued legal action against Pictopia.com. The TV tabloids were all over it, and within a week the number of people who viewed that picture, which she did not want seen, had increased from 4 to 420,000.

Just to confirm this as the ultimate entertainment example of the Cobra Effect, Streisand lost the lawsuit. As the story took legs, a variation of the term was established. If a celebrity with valid intentions initiated an attempt to solve a problem which resulted in unintended results creating a much huger problem than originally existed it became known as the "Streisand Effect."

THE GREAT HANOI RAT MASSACRE OF 1902 ~ As we sway through this piece on the Cobra Effect, we are going to meander from entertainment back to history. This Vietnamese adventure is generally considered to be the second most historically significant example of the

Cobra Effect, behind only the original event which we shared with you earlier. There is one telling similarity between these two situations. They both involve European colonial powers operating in Asian countries with a somewhat annoying air of arrogance that comes back to bite them in the ass.

The anti-hero of our story this week is a Frenchman named Paul Doumer. While serving as Minister of Finance during the 1890's Doumer tried to implement an income tax plan which was an utter failure. His "reward" for this was an all-expense-paid, five-year vacation in Vietnam where he did get to serve as Governor-General of French Indochina, the name by which the colony was referred to at that time. Apparently, the thought process was, "If he's going to screw something up, let's have it be on another continent." During his time in Vietnam, Doumer was able to add to his resumé being the mastermind behind the Great Hanoi Rat Massacre.

As was usually the case during this era of colonialism, the French people lived high on the hog while exploiting the native Vietnamese. While the natives mostly lived in huts, the European Aristocracy resided in affluent French style villas with all the amenities. But the one thing that they did not have was toilets and Doumer made it his mission to, come hell or high water, enable the French to flush.

OUT WITH THE OUTHOUSES ~ To this end he had Vietnamese workers dig trenches and install nine miles of sewer lines below the French section of town in Hanoi. Prior to this, Vietnam had been relatively rat free. Sure, there were a few rummaging around looking for food in the trashy area of the city, but once Doumer completed the sewer system those ghetto rats started movin' on up to the glamorous side of town. What the French had inadvertently done was create a dark and super cool rodent paradise where they could travel and breed without the fear of predators and use their subterranean superhighway to access the city's ritziest trash cans. Subsequently the rat population of French Hanoi exploded.

So Doumer found himself in familiar territory, namely the dog house. Subsequently he came up with a plan. The French government hired Vietnamese rat hunters who were sent down into the sewers and paid on a per-rat basis to eliminate the pesky pests. Talk about your adverse working conditions. Ironically, the files which had the most extensive French documentation of the Rat Massacre were not rediscovered until the 1990's and they included some mind-blowing statistics. Listen to these numbers. The first documented death toll was for the last week of April, 1902 when 7,985 rats were killed. Let the games begin.

RAT STATS ~ The tally for May 1902 was over 125,000 dead rats, with May 30 being the single most deadly day –15,041. The harvest for June was around 300,000 with a single day record of 20,112 being achieved on June 21. How these numbers were determined is not specified in the French documentation but the conjecture is that the corpses were weighed en masse and then the total weight divided by the average weight of one rat to arrive at a specific number. Any way you cut the cheese, there were some folks performing some nasty jobs back then.

The following is a quote taken from the French documentation which serves as a job description for the paid rat killers. "One had to enter the dark and cramped sewer system, make one's way through human waste in various forms of decay, and hunt down a relatively fierce wild animal which could be carrying fleas with the bubonic plague or other contagious diseases. This is not even to mention the probable existence of numerous other dangerous animals, such as snakes, spiders, and other creatures, that make our skin crawl with anxiety."

And now are you ready for the bad news? The rats were holding their own. Despite the hundreds of thousands that had been killed, the rat population was basically maintaining itself on a consistent level. So at this point Doumer proceeded to enact his plan B. Apparently unaware of what happened to the British in India, the French introduced a bounty system which was available to every Vietnamese citizen, not just the government-hired rat catchers.

BRING ON THE BOUNTY ~ Perhaps enlisting the assistance of enterprising civilians could help tip the scales. The bounty was set at a profitable per rat price and all you had to do to collect your reward was provide the rat's tail to a municipal office, thus avoiding the government problem of figuring out how to dispose of even more rat corpses.

Doumer and the French government were proud of the program because it seemed to align with the stated desire to encourage entrepreneurialism amongst the Vietnamese. The initial results were encouraging. There were trails of tails being turned in at the municipal offices and prideful boasts that French ingenuity had prevailed again.

FRENCH FRIED ~ But it wasn't long after the French were toasting their success that the French realized they had just become toast. This tragic transition was the result of a strange phenomenon seen running about the streets of French Hanoi. Okay, you guessed it, rats. But not just any rats. These were robust rats running around with NO TAILS!

The French had been duped and the motivation was obvious. Remember the civilian hunters did not have to produce a complete body; they could earn the bounty by turning in just the tail. And amputating the tail had a twofold benefit for the bounty hunters: #1) It was quicker and easier to just cut off the tail; and, #2) They were cutting off their tails not their testicles. The tailless rats were free to scurry back into the sewer, procreate, and send forth a whole new generation of rats with tails that could be lopped off for the bounty.

So the French had been fried and fraudulently freed of their francs. Classic Cobra Effect, a seemingly logical solution to a problem ironically exacerbates the situation, resulting in the unintended consequence that the problem becomes even worse than it was before.

WINS & LOSSES ~ Just to provide closure, we'll end the story with a final update on Paul Doumer. After leaving Vietnam and returning to his native France, his life had some ups and downs. On the plus side he thrived politically and was actually elected President of France. He had eight children, five boys and three girls, but on the down side all five of his sons died in WWI and in 1932 he became the only French President ever to be assassinated. You win some; you lose some.

FOOTNOTES

CHAPTER 2

[1] Howard Cohen, "Restless Souls: The Tate Family's Crusade to Keep the Manson Killers Behind Bars," *popMATTERS*, accessed January 8, 2019, https://www.popmatters.com/156233-restless-souls-2495870089.html

CHAPTER 3

[1] "The Manson Sessions", *Manson Family Blog*, accessed March 3, 2019 http://www.mansonblog.com/2017/05/the-manson-sessions.html

[2] "Untitled Charles Manson Project (late 60's, unreleased recordings)," *Lost Media Archive*, accessed January 10, 2019, https://lostmediaarchive.fandom.com/wiki/Untitled_Charles_Manson_Project_(late_60%27s,_unreleased_recordings)

[3] "Untitle Charles Manson Project (late 60's, unreleased recordings)," *Lost Media Archive*, accessed January 10, 2019, https://lostmediaarchive.fandom.com/wiki/Untitled_Charles_Manson_Project_(late_60%27s,_unreleased_recordings)

[4] Vincent Bugliosi, *Helter Skelter* (New York, NY: W.W. Norton & Company Inc., 1974), 251

CHAPTER 6

[1] Douglas O. Linder, "The Influence of the Beatles on Charles Manson," *Famous Trials*, accessed February 4, 2019, http://www.famous-trials.com/manson/244-influence

[2] Bianca Barragan, "Mapping 13 Key Locations in the 1969 Manson Family Murders," *Curbed Los Angeles*, accessed January 12, 2019 https://la.curbed.com/maps/charles-manson-sharon-tate-prison

[3] Rikka Agtarap, Adrian Valencia & Mirna Cabrera, "Mr. Tripp: Manson Family Cult," *Slideshare*, accessed January 14, 2019, https://www.slideshare.net/MirnaCabrera01/the-manson-family

CHAPTER 7

[1] Susan Atkins with Bob Slosser *Child of Satan, Child of God* 21,000 (Plainfield, NJ: Logos International, 1977), page

[2] Spencer J. and Pamela T. Atkinson, *Proof From the Light and Darkness,* https://books.google.com/books?id=sg6WhYpCutoC&pg=PA82&lpg=PA82&dq=It+looks+like+we're+gonna+have+to+show+blackie+how+to+do+it.%E2%80%9D&source=bl&ots=ilK3SC874B&sig=ACfU3U1LYd3bpwMQtQLdgp8Lmbbm5vlebA&hl=en&sa=X&ved=2ahUKEwiatNLy-tngAhVrUN8KHfLuCt4Q6AEwAnoECAMQAQ#v=onepage&q=It%20looks%20like%20we're%20gonna%20have%20to%20show%20blackie%20how%20to%20do%20it.%E2%80%9D&f=false

[3] Michael Merle Thomas, *Manson's Last Disciple*, accessed January 19, 2019, https://books.google.com/books?id=EupwDwAAQBAJ&pg=PT27&lpg=PT27&dq= manson+says,+%22It's+time+for+Helter+Skelter%22&source=bl&ots=myt8eLokBS &sig=ACfU3U0enFfyhBiLHo49K9DJE3SCKBSwWg&hl=en&sa=X&ved=2ahUKE wjutYqnhO7gAhVC3IMKHVSRCjYQ6AEwAHoECAEQAQ#v=onepage&q=mans on%20says%2C%20%22It's%20time%20for%20Helter%20Skelter%22&f=false.

[4] Vincent Bugliosi, *Helter Skelter* (New York, NY: W.W. Norton & Company Inc., 1974), 465

[5] Lis Wiehl, "The Quest For Justice in the Days of Helter Skelter," *Hunting Charles Manson*, accessed February 1, 2019. https://books.google.com/books?id=Dyk-DwAAQBAJ&pg=PA35&dq=Do+what+Tex+says.+Leave+a+sign.+You+girls+know+ what+I+mean,+something+witchy.%E2%80%9D&hl=en&sa=X&ved=0ahUKEwiKp rXH_dngAhWnmeAKHQkmDLEQ6AEIKjAA#v=onepage&q=Do%20what%20Te x%20says.%20Leave%20a%20sign.%20You%20girls%20know%20what%20I%20 mean%2C%20something%20witchy.%E2%80%9D&f=false

[6] Joel Whitburn, "Eagles," *Top Pop Singles 1955-1986* (Menomonee Falls, WI: Record Research Inc. 1987) 161

CHAPTER 8

[1] Vincent Bugliosi, *Helter Skelter* (New York, NY: W.W. Norton & Company Inc., 1974), 4

[2] Rob Kirkpatrick, *1969: The Year Everything Changed*, accessed January 28, 2019, https://books.google.com/books?id=sURrP5uKQI0C&pg=PA158&dq=I%E2%80% 99m+the+devil.+and+I%E2%80%99m+here+to+do+the+devil%E2%80%99s+busine ss&hl=en&sa=X&ved=0ahUKEwji_-r0idrgAhWMdd8KHR6NA54Q6AEINDAC#v=onepage&q=I%E2%80%99m%20t he%20devil%2C%20and%20I%E2%80%99m%20here%20to%20do%20the%20d evil%E2%80%99s%20business&f=false.

[3] "Susan Atkins," *RXSTR*, accessed February 2, 2019, https://rxstr.com/tag/susan-atkins/

[4] Susan Atkins, *Child of Satan, Child of God* (Plainfield, New Jersey: Logos International, 1977), 144

CHAPTER 9

[1] Susan Atkins, *Child of Satan, Child of God* (Plainfield, New Jersey: Logos International, 1977), 145

[2] Douglas O. Linder, "Kill the Driver on Way to the LaBiancas, Testimony of Linda Kasabian" *Famous Trials*, accessed February 4, 2019, http://www.famous-trials.com/manson/257-lindatestimony

CHAPTER 10

[1] "Charles Manson," *Very Scary People*, CNN, March 17, 2019

[2] "Charles Manson," *Very Scary People*, CNN, March 17, 2019

[3] Susan Atkins, *Child of Satan, Child of God* (Plainfield, New Jersey: Logos International, 1977), 149.

[4]Susan Atkins, *Child of Satan, Child of God* (Plainfield, New Jersey: Logos International, 1977), 149.

[5]"Linda Kasabian Testified Manson Ordered Her to Kill Actor," *CieloDrive.com*, accessed February 6, 2019, www.cielodrive.com/archive/linda-kasabian-testifies-manson-ordered-her-to-kill-actor/

CHAPTER 11

[1]"Police Raid Ranch, Arrest 26 Suspects in Auto Theft Ring", "Anatomy of a Mass Murder in Hollywood", "LaBianca Couple, Victims of Slayer Given Final Rites", *Los Angeles Times*, August 17, 1969

[2]Vincent Bugliosi, *Helter Skelter* (New York, NY: W.W. Norton & Company Inc., 1974), 20

[3]Steven V. Roberts, "Charles Manson: One Man's Family," *New York Times* (New York, NY), January 4, 1970

[4]Gene Maddaus, "Judge Skeptical of Roman Polanski Latest Bid to End 40-Year-Old Rape Case," *Variety.com*, accessed January 30, 2019, https://variety.com/2017/biz/news/roman-polanski-rape-case-harland-braun-extradition-1202011822/

[5]Vincent Bugliosi, *Helter Skelter* (New York, NY: W.W. Norton & Company Inc., 1974), 57

CHAPTER 12

[1]Vincent Bugliosi, *Helter Skelter* (New York, NY: W.W. Norton & Company Inc., 1974), 82

[2]Vincent Bugliosi, *Helter Skelter* (New York, NY: W.W. Norton & Company Inc., 1974), 371

[3]Vincent Bugliosi, *Helter Skelter* (New York, NY: W.W. Norton & Company Inc., 1974), 197

CHAPTER 13

[1]"People V Manson," *Justia US Law*, accessed February 7, 2019, https://law.justia.com/cases/california/court-of-appeal/3d/71/1.html

[2]Vincent Bugliosi, *Helter Skelter* (New York, NY: W.W. Norton & Company Inc., 1974), 265

[3]"Summation of Prosecutor Vincent Bugliosi in the Charles Manson (Tate-LaBianca Murder) Trial," *Famous Truals.com*, accessed February 13, 2019, http://famous-trials.com/legacyftrials/manson/mansonsummation.html

[4]"Summation of Prosecutor Vincent Bugliosi in the Charles Manson (Tate-LaBianca Murder) Trial," *Famous Truals.com*, accessed February 13, 2019, http://famous-trials.com/legacyftrials/manson/mansonsummation.html

[5] Jeff Guinn, *Manson: The Life and Times of Charles Manson*, 353 https://books.google.com/books?id=RC9Rr1YVLdsC&pg=PA353&lpg=PA353&dq=%E2%80%9Cthere+is+a+minimum+of+client+control+in+this+case.%E2%80%9D++paul+fitzgerald+manson&source=bl&ots=Af0SaSYSta&sig=ACfU3U2fwGC8lD8KIbChanxlHIAeVoDc6A&hl=en&sa=X&ved=2ahUKE

wjl6Jn52drgAhXkY98KHahLBocQ6AEwAHoECAEQAQ#v=onepage&q=%E2%80%9
Cthere%20is%20a%20minimum%20of%20client%20control%20in%20this%20cas
e.%E2%80%9D%20%20paul%20fitzgerald%20manson&f=false

[6]"People V Manson," *Justia US Law*, accessed February 7, 2019,
https://law.justia.com/cases/california/court-of-appeal/3d/61/102.html

[7]"Charles Manson - Quotes Throughout the Years Concerning the Trial and Media,"
MansonDirect,

https://www.mansondirect.com/quotes-cm.html

[8]"Little Known Facts About Manson Crimes," *Real Clear History*, accessed January 30,
2019,
www.realclearhistory.com/2017/01/25/little_known_facts_about_manson_crimes_13
52.html?mobile_redirect=true

[9]"Little Known Facts About Manson Crimes," *Real Clear History*, accessed January 30,
2019,
www.realclearhistory.com/2017/01/25/little_known_facts_about_manson_crimes_13
52.html?mobile_redirect=true

[10] Vincent Bugliosi, *Helter Skelter* (New York, NY: W.W. Norton & Company Inc.,
1974), 303.

CHAPTER 14

[1]Vincent Bugliosi, *Helter Skelter* (New York, NY: W.W. Norton & Company Inc., 1974),
306

[2]Vincent Bugliosi, *Helter Skelter* (New York, NY: W.W. Norton & Company Inc., 1974),
306

[3]"Charles Manson Never Killed Anyone," *KnowledgeNuts*, accessed February 14, 2019,
https://knowledgenuts.com/2013/07/20/charles-manson-never-killed-anyone/

[4]Douglas O Linder, "The Charles Manson (Tate-LaBianca Murder) Trial," *Famous Trials*,
accessed February 6, 2019, https://www.famous-trials.com/manson/243-home

CHAPTER 15

[1]"Bugliosi's opening statement," CeiloDrive.com, accessed January 18, 2019,
http://www.cielodrive.com/updates/vincent-bugliosis-opening-statement/

[2] "Bugliosi's opening statement," CeiloDrive.Com, accessed January 18, 2019,
http://www.cielodrive.com/updates/vincent-bugliosis-opening-statement/

[3]"William Garretson Testimony," *Charles Manson-The True Story*, accessed January 25,
2019, https://www.charlesmanson.com/testimony/william-garretson-testimony/

CHAPTER 16

[1]"Manson Girls," *RXSTR*, accessed February 9, 2019, https://rxstr.com/tag/manson-
girls/page/2/

[2] John Kendall, "Mrs. Kasabian's Testimony Met by 50 Defense Objections,"
Newspapers.com, accessed February 26, 2019,
https://www.newspapers.com/clip/24459529/the_los_angeles_times/.

[3]Douglas O Linder, "The Charles Manson (Tate-LaBianca Murder) Trial," *Famous Trials*,
accessed February 6, 2019, https://www.famous-trials.com/manson/243-home.

[4]Douglas O Linder, "The Charles Manson (Tate-LaBianca Murder) Trial," *Famous Trials*, accessed February 6, 2019, https:// https://www.famous-trials.com/manson/250-keyfigures

[5]Douglas O Linder, "The Charles Manson (Tate-LaBianca Murder) Trial," *Famous Trials*, accessed February 6, 2019, https:// https://www.famous-trials.com/manson/250-keyfigures

[6] Douglas O Linder "Obeying Charlie: Famous Trials Testimony of Linda Kasabian in the Charles Manson Trial, *Famous Trials*, accessed February 7, 2019, https://www.famous-trials.com/manson/257-lindatestimony

[7]Vincent Bugliosi, *Helter Skelter* (New York, NY: W.W. Norton & Company Inc., 1974), 322

[8]Leopold N. Loeb, "Nixon Calls Manson Guilty; Attorneys Move a Mistrial," *Harvard Crimson*,   accessed February 13, 2019, https://www.thecrimson.com/article/1970/8/4/nixon-calls-manson-guilty-attorneys-move/

[9]Leopold N. Loeb, "Nixon Calls Manson Guilty; Attorneys Move a Mistrial," *Harvard Crimson*, accessed February 13, 2019, https://www.thecrimson.com/article/1970/8/4/nixon-calls-manson-guilty-attorneys-move/

[10]Leopold N. Loeb, "Nixon Calls Manson Guilty; Attorneys Move a Mistrial," *Harvard Crimson*, accessed February 13, 2019, https://www.thecrimson.com/article/1970/8/4/nixon-calls-manson-guilty-attorneys-move/

[11]Leopold N. Loeb, "Nixon Calls Manson Guilty; Attorneys Move a Mistrial," *Harvard Crimson*, accessed February 13, 2019, https://www.thecrimson.com/article/1970/8/4/nixon-calls-manson-guilty-attorneys-move/

CHAPTER 17

[1]"Murder Victim's Picture Shakes Up State Witness," *CieloDrive.com*, accessed February 22, 2019, https://www.cielodrive.com/archive/murder-victims-picture-shakes-up-state-witness/

[2]"Murder Victim's Picture Shakes Up State Witness," *CieloDrive.com*, accessed February 22, 2019, https://www.cielodrive.com/archive/murder-victims-picture-shakes-up-state-witness/

[3]Susan Atkins, *Child of Satan, Child of God* (Plainfield, New Jersey: Logos International, 1977), 166

[4]"Vincent Bugliosi, Helter Skelter (New York, NY: W.W. Norton & Company Inc., 1974), 331

[5]"Vincent Bugliosi, Helter Skelter (New York, NY: W.W. Norton & Company Inc., 1974), 331

[6]"Vincent Bugliosi, Helter Skelter (New York, NY: W.W. Norton & Company Inc., 1974), 330

CHAPTER 18

[1]Douglas O Linder, "Testimony of Charles Manson in the Tate-LaBianca Murder Trial,"

Famous Trials, accessed February 11, 2019, https://www.famous-trials.com/manson/258-mansontestimony

[2]"A Psychedelic Hamburger Helped Convict Charles Manson," *Atlas Obscura*, accessed January 16, 2019, https://www.atlasobscura.com/articles/psychedelic-hamburger-lsd-charles-manson-witness-attempted-murder

[3]"A Psychedelic Hamburger Helped Convict Charles Manson," *Atlas Obscura*, accessed January 16, 2019, https://www.atlasobscura.com/articles/psychedelic-hamburger-lsd-charles-manson-witness-attempted-murder.

[4]"Charles Manson: The True Story," *CharlesManson.com*, accessed February 24, 2019, https://www.charlesmanson.com/related/straight-satans/

[5]"Danny DeCarlo," *CieloDrive.com*, accessed February 9, 2019, http://www.cielodrive.com/daniel-decarlo.php

[6]"Testimony of Danny DeCarlo About Tex," *Tripod*, accessed February 11, 2019, http://members.tripod.com/dark_veil_of_dusk/id57.html

[7]Martin Waldron, "Witness Recalls Manson as 'Devil'," *NewYorkTimes.com*, accessed February 16, 2019, https://www.nytimes.com/1970/09/18/archives/witness-recalls-manson-as-devil-he-says-murder-defendant-posed-as.html

CHAPTER 19

[1]"DeCarlo's Testimony," *Tripod*, accessed February 23, 2019, http://members.tripod.com/*dark*_veil_of_dusk/id57.html.

[2] "Juan Flynn," *Charles Manson: The True Story,* accessed February 27, 2019, https://www.charlesmanson.com/related/juan-flynn/

[3]"Charles Manson Trial: 1970-71," *Great American Trials*, accessed February 24, 2019, https://www.encyclopedia.com/people/social-sciences-and-law/crime-and-law-enforcement-biographies/charles-manson

[4]"Juan Flynn," *Charles Manson: The True Story,* accessed February 27, 2019, https://www.charlesmanson.com/related/juan-flynn/

[5]"People V Manson," *Justia US Law,* accessed February 7, 2019, https://law.justia.com/cases/california/court-of-appeal/3d/61/102.html

[6]Martin Waldron, "Manson Leaps at Judge in the Tate Murder Trial and Declares 'Someone Should Cut Your Head Off'," *NewYorkTimes.com*, accessed February 3, 2019, https://www.nytimes.com/1970/10/06/archives/manson-leaps-at-judge-in-the-tate-murder-trial-and-declares-someone.html

[7]Diane Bartz, Steve Gorman, "Mass killer, cult leader Charles Manson dies at 83," *Reuters*, accessed January 13, 2019, https://www.reuters.com/article/us-people-charlesmanson/mass-killer-cult-leader-charles-manson-dies-at-83-idUSKBN1DK0JD

CHAPTER 20

[1]"The 1970 Death of Ronald Hughes: Manson Family Defence Attorney Vanishes and is Found Dead During Their Trial," *Unresolved Mysteries,* accessed January 17, 2019, https://www.reddit.com/r/UnresolvedMysteries/comments/7nu8e5/the_1970_death_of_ronald_hughes_manson_family/

[2]"Testimony of Charles Manson in the Tate-LaBianca Murder Trial," *Famous Trials*, accessed February 28, 2019, https://www.famous-trials.com/manson/258-mansontestimony

[3]Vincent Bugliosi, *Helter Skelter* (New York, NY: W.W. Norton & Company Inc., 1974), 393

[4]"Tate Trial Delayed to Dec. 16," *CieloDrive.com*, accessed February 9, 2019, http://www.cielodrive.com/archive/tate-trial-delayed-to-dec-16/

[5]"Maxwell S. Keith Dies at 87; Replacement Lawyer in Manson Case," *New York Times.com*, accessed February 11, 2019, https://www.nytimes.com/2012/03/11/us/maxwell-s-keith-lawyer-in-manson-case-dies-at-87.html

CHAPTER 21

[1]"The Manson Story: Love and Murder," *CieloDrive.com*, accessed January 31, 2019 http://www.cielodrive.com/archive/the-manson-story-love-and-murder/

[2] Jeff Guinn, *Manson: The Life and Times of Charles Manson,* 353 https://books.google.com/books?id=RC9Rr1YVLdsC&pg=PA353&lpg=PA353&dq=%E2%80%9Cthere+is+a+minimum+of+client+control+in+this+case.%E2%80%9D++paul+fitzgerald+manson&source=bl&ots=Af0SaSYSta&sig=ACfU3U2fwGC8lD8KIbChanxlHIAeVoDc6A&hl=en&sa=X&ved=2ahUKEwjl6Jn52drgAhXkY98KHahLBocQ6AEwAHoECAEQAQ#v=onepage&q=%E2%80%9Cthere%20is%20a%20minimum%20of%20client%20control%20in%20this%20case.%E2%80%9D%20%20paul%20fitzgerald%20manson&f=false

[3]"Charles Manson Trial: 1970-71 - Jury Convicts All Defendants," accessed February 23, 2019, http://law.jrank.org/pages/3204/Charles-Manson-Trial-1970-71-Jury-Convicts-All-Defendants.html

[4]"Manson Girls Acid Trips are Detailed," *CieloDrive.com*, accessed February 17, 2019 http://www.cielodrive.com/archive/manson-girls-acid-trips-detailed/

[5]"Manson Girls Acid Trips are Detailed," *CieloDrive.com*, accessed February 17, 2019 http://www.cielodrive.com/archive/manson-girls-acid-trips-detailed/

[6]Peter Levenda, Sinister Forces: *A Grimoire of American Political Witchcraft, Book Two: A Warm Gun*, accessed February 24, 2019, https://books.google.com/books?id=nP0BBAAAQBAJ&pg=PT137&lpg=PT137&dq=Kanarek+Manson+Easter+in+trial&source=bl&ots=uY8R0zSPmR&sig=ACfU3U1IuODSkZCBKI3Ul2wIOwFJWnnjGQ&hl=en&sa=X&ved=2ahUKEwieqOO30O7gAhUCU98KHUymAP0Q6AEwDHoECAIQAQ#v=onepage&q=Kanarek%20Manson%20Easter%20in%20trial&f=false

[7]Vincent Bugliosi, *Helter Skelter* (New York, NY: W.W. Norton & Company Inc., 1974), 454

[8]"March 18-29, 1971," Indbooks, accessed February 26, 2019, http://indbooks.in/mirror1/?p=318767

CHAPTER 22

[1] Jack Godwin, "Infamous cult leader Charles Manson is dead at 83," *VT*, accessed February 11, 2019, http://vt.co/news/us/infamous-cult-leader-charles-manson-dead-83/

[2] "The Manson Story: Love and Murder," *CieloDrive*, accessed February 27, 2019, http://www.cielodrive.com/archive/the-manson-story-love-and-murder/

[3] Douglas O Linder, "The Charles Manson (Tate-LaBianca Murder) Trial," *Famous Trials*, accessed February 13, 2019, https://www.famous-trials.com/manson/243-home

[4] "Susan Atkins 1948-2009," *The Week*, accessed February 26, 2019, https://theweek.com/articles/501388/susan-atkins

[5] "Parole Hearing For Leslie Van Houten," *CieloDrive.com*, accessed February 4, 2019, http://www.cielodrive.com/leslie-van-houten-parole-hearing-2013.php

[6] Vincent Bugliosi, *Helter Skelter* (New York, NY: W.W. Norton & Company Inc., 1974), - Jury awards

[7] Theo Wilson, "Charles Manson and followers sentenced to death in 1971 for killing actress Sharon Tate and six others," *NewYorkDailyNews.com*, accessed February 19, 2019, https://www.nydailynews.com/news/crime/charles-manson-followers-sentenced-death-1971-article-1.2581343

[8] Vincent Bugliosi, *Helter Skelter* (New York, NY: W.W. Norton & Company Inc., 1974), 458

[9] "Crim. No. 13617. Supreme Court of California. February 18, 1972," *Stanford Law School*, accessed February 24, 2019 https://scocal.stanford.edu/opinion/people-v-anderson-22750

[10] Susan Atkins, *Child of Satan, Child of God* (Plainfield, New Jersey: Logos International, 1977), 182

CHAPTER 23

[1] "Charles Manson New Worth," Celebrity New Worth, accessed February 19, 2019, https://www.celebritynetworth.com/richest-businessmen/richest-criminals/charles-manson-net-worth/

[2] Karen Bennett, "How Charles Manson and Other Serial Killers Made Money in Jail," *Cheatsheet*, accessed March 8, 2019, https://www.cheatsheet.com/money-career/how-charles-manson-and-other-serial-killers-made-money-in-jail.html/

ABOUT THE AUTHORS

We have a rather unique back story, most of which is set in upstate New York. We met on the first day of high school, brought together by the merger of two neighboring school districts. We ended up dating for all four years of high school, then went to different colleges and, as fate would have it, we ended up not seeing each other again for literally 40 years.

Tim's mom passed away in late 2012 and Deb heard about it through the grapevine in Virginia Beach where she was teaching. She sent him a sympathy card, he wrote back, one thing led to another and Tim ended up coming down to Virginia Beach in June of 2013 to pick Deb up after her school year ended and bringing her back to New York.

The thing Deb remembers most from that courtship period when she was in Virginia, but longing to be back in New York, was that every day at school when she went to her mailbox, there was an envelope from Tim. And each one contained an original letter Deb had written to him 40 years ago. He had saved every one. His go-to line regarding that part of the story is to say, "Yeah, it took me a long time to play those cards!" Sometimes the best things in life are worth waiting for.

We got engaged on Deb's mother's birthday (December 4, 2014) and we got married on Tim's mother's birthday (June 12, 2015). Because we both have Native American ancestry, we had the ceremony performed at the Ganondagan Historic Site by the Native American leader there, as well as a former student of Tim's.

So how did we get into this writing gig? Well, as fate would have it, we happen to live right next door to the newspaper office in our town. After hearing some of our stories, the publisher of the paper, Chris Carosa, suggested we write something for the paper. So we started by telling the personal story of our relationship and we haven't stopped writing since. Currently our weekly feature comprises the entire back page of the *Mendon-Honeoye Falls-Lima Sentinel*.

We write about an eclectic variety of topics including music, sports, travel and human interest. Our publisher has been encouraging us to write a book for some time now and we had been waiting for a topic to emerge about which we felt we could apply our own irreverent style. Despite the tragic nature of the story, we felt that we put a unique perspective on the story of *The Beatles, the Bible & Manson: Reflecting Back with 50 Years of Perspective*.

We hope you enjoyed it.

THE BEATLES, THE BIBLE & MANSON

If you liked our book, there's lots more where that came from. Sign up for

Tim & Deb's Superfan Kit # 1

To receive the following bonus items

* Timeline of Important Events
* Manson Family Christmas Album
* Limericks, Songs & Poems
* Open Letter from Manson to Hitler
* Our Analysis of Police Ineptitude
* Abridged Version for Slow Readers
* The Original Book Review
* Tim/Deb photo ~ replica signatures

Just go to eBay and search for "Tim & Deb's Superfan Kit #1" and you'll connect directly to our eBay store.